This book is dedicated to the memory of
Stan Drawdy
May 5, 1954—September 28, 2022

Just as the book was completed and ready for printing, Stan passed away. He was dedicated to the idea of this book, and was eager to hold it in his hands. Now, as we hold this book in our hands, we can think of Stan with love and appreciation for his life, and for all his efforts to make this book possible. Without him, it would not have happened.

Keith Carter

Contents

Acknowledgments

The idea of this book had for some time been in the mind of Ingram Truluck, who had wanted to see the growing-up years of his neighborhood's generation memorialized. He had conversations about it with Keith Carter and others over the years, but things never got past the talking stage. That is, until Stan Drawdy distinguished himself by writing a book of his own, *My Dad...My Father*. That's what was needed—someone with the pioneering spirit, the credentials, and the know-how that had been lacking. Ingram enlisted the help of his sister, Barbara Truluck Benjamin, who was instrumental in collecting the names and contact information of potential contributors to this book. Once Stan got the operation underway, Keith Carter was asked to lend a hand, and he eagerly joined the effort to pull the book together into publishing form. It was a combined labor of love!

From left to right: Ingram Truluck, Keith Carter, Stan Drawdy, and Barbara Truluck Benjamin.
Final planning session, May 2022

The contributors who wrote the contents of this volume are ordinary citizens who lived at least a portion of their lives on or near Greenway Drive in Darlington, South Carolina. Most of them were children during the 1950s and 1960s while growing up there, but some are of the generation of parents of those children. If the call for memories and stories had been issued years earlier, there would surely have been many more memories submitted by parents—those members of the Greatest Generation who are no longer with us. We cannot turn back the hands of time, but we can surely remember with great love and respect those who chose to raise families in our cherished neighborhood and are now gone. They are certainly not forgotten, and many of them are mentioned in this book.

Most, if not all, who contributed to this book are now senior citizens themselves! We trust that all have perfect memories of their antics and the events from sixty or so years ago that they wrote about, as their words are their bond! Some still live on Greenway Drive or in the area, while some live in other parts of South Carolina, and others in distant states. As can be seen, this was a group effort, and every contribution is appreciated. We hope it is obvious to any reader that a great time was had by all of the contributors during the years covered in this book!

Introduction

In the town of Darlington, South Carolina, there is a street named Greenway Drive. There is nothing outwardly special or different about this street, which is not long and is actually a dead-end street; but it is special to people who call(ed) it theirs. This collection of memories and stories was written by people who lived or grew up on or near Greenway Drive, including Evans Street and Circle, Pinehaven Avenue, and the section of Spring Street between Greenway and Pinehaven. We do think our neighborhood was special, as we hope the words in this book will demonstrate. All organizations that are worth their salt have one thing in common: good people. It was "the people" that made our neighborhood so special! We were fortunate enough to grow up during a time when people were important! It was a time when the family unit was the glue that held everything together.

Greenway Drive existed before World War II, but it became active during the baby boom years that followed the war—those record-breaking years from 1946 to 1964, during which three million to four million babies were born annually in this country. Young American men and women celebrated the end of the war by getting married, starting families, and beginning careers. Those new couples had grown up in the Great Depression, which was followed by the world's most destructive war. The ensuing peace and prosperity in our country was well worth celebrating, and the people eagerly turned their backs on hard times and war. In many ways, our neighborhood was like many others in this country. But we think the events that went on in our neighborhood were worthy of being shared. As you read, keep in mind that this was the 1950s and 1960s. We were free-range children, but our range was not very far or wide, especially in our single-digit years. We had lots of mothers watching out for us as we walked, ran, pedaled, and skated up and down Greenway Drive. We played in and around creeks and ponds, climbed trees, caught snakes, built huts and tree houses, played house, played ball, raced bicycles, skinned knees and elbows, went barefoot, teased and got teased, laughed, and cried.

Yes, included here are some of the pranks and hijinks that were played during our years in the neighborhood. You will read about our laughter and tears, the dangers we faced, and our victories and failures. But more than that, you will read about our love and acceptance of each other; our becoming team players; the beginnings of lifelong friendships; the shaping of our personalities; and our differences, talents, and abilities. In adulthood, many became leaders and professionals as well as parents and grandparents who understand childhood and life. We learned to trust and, more importantly, to be trustworthy. We learned to care about each other, to get along and (usually) live in harmony with everyone in the neighborhood. We became good citizens. Thank God for those years, lessons, and friends.

At suppertime, we sat at a table and talked about what we learned at school and (some of) what we had done that day. We didn't know what being bored was—we knew how to have fun! It was a very homogeneous neighborhood—the residents were generally all of the same ages, of the same middle class, and with similar backgrounds. It made it a fun, healthy, convivial, cohesive, and upwardly mobile place to live. We created our own events, organized them, and ran them. We played ball with no referees, umpires, or fans. We raced—everything! We knew the rules and boundaries and were able to operate within those most of the time.

The point of all this is simply to say that we grew up in a neighborhood where there was love within the families and between the families. Things were not perfect, and sometimes we didn't get along, but somehow it always seemed to work out. The very fact that twenty-one people have written about their memories and their love of this small neighborhood, after long years have passed, should indicate the impact it made on our lives forever. Our neighborhood was a great place to live and to grow up, and these are our words!

Stan Drawdy (then and now)

Keith Carter (then and now)

Sarah Cain Spruill

The View from the
Top of the Street

My father, William Cain, came to Darlington in the 1930s to teach, partly because the state tennis tournament was held in Darlington. He, with the help of some of the St. John's High School shop boys, built the beginnings of our house on the front of the block bounded by what became Greenway Drive and Spring Street Extension. There were no other houses close by. Our house was built on the site of an old honky-tonk, and we used to find broken bottles in the garden all the time. He picked this site because of the massive Darlington Oak in the backyard and the view over the pond to Williamson Park.

My parents were a good bit older than most of the parents in the neighborhood. Daddy was the principal at St. John's High, and Mother was the guidance counselor. He married my mother, Mary Jane, who had also come to Darlington to teach, during the war. When they returned from his service in the Army, they added a bedroom. When I was six, they added another bedroom, larger kitchen, and dining room, making a long white house on top of the hill. They planted the bank with daffodils, day lilies, and flowering trees. Daddy brought lots of bulbs from Somerset, the plantation he grew up on. My brother Billy (William Jr.) was born in January 1947, and I was born in February of 1948. We were the first of the baby boomers, and what a wave was to follow, filling the streets and yards of Greenway Drive.

We called our mother "Honey" because Daddy always called her that. I think that Mr. T. E. Wilson owned all of the property that became Greenway Drive, Evans Street, and "the Other Street," as we always called it. When we were very young, Dr. John Wilson and his family lived at the very end of Greenway Drive. I vaguely remember when the small houses were built on Greenway Drive and when the chain gang paved the street. Wagons still occasionally came in from the country on Spring Street. In our childhood, there were two bridges across Swift Creek, both with wooden planks that rattled when something crossed them. We played a good bit down there, sailing watermelon boats and racing leaf boats under the bridges. I clearly remember when someone dumped a giant dead snapping turtle there. It smelled awful. We would often hear the hoot of owls in the night and the terrifying screech of wildcats from time to time. Raccoon and other animal tracks were found along the stream banks.

When we were very small, there was always an adult around or various maids with babies, keeping a general eye on things. I remember riding our tricycles on the dirt street between the Sansburys and the Bonnoitts. I think it was the Bonnoitts' new puppy that chased us, biting at our heels. The puppy became ill, and they found it had rabies. All of us—I think I was three—had to take rabies shots which were given in your stomach. Mama said that one night I rolled on my tummy and mumbled in my sleep, "I hate those dern it, dammit dogs." There was an artesian well or "flowing well" at the bottom of our yard. The water was always cold there. Daddy grew Siberian Iris along that little stream. We had several tree houses in the woodsy part of the yard. We were always building something. One of the tree houses went across the driveway there, but our parents made us take it down, I think for fear of a child falling out right in front of a car. We were quite annoyed. The huge oak in the backyard came down during a storm. I remember Billy and me hiding under the bed when that happened. It took Daddy and James, the yard man, quite a while to cut that tree up with a crosscut saw. In the meantime, it became our jungle gym, our pirate ship, our airplane.

The first families I remember on the street were the Jim Browns, the David Browns, the Bonnoitts, the Sansburys, the Carters, Mrs.

Kirven, the Mills, the Jeffords, and the Richard Johnsons. Almost every family had children. Billy's best friend was Coke Jeffords, who I also loved because he was kind to me, the little sister. Coke was a year older than Billy. He had an older brother, Joe; their dad worked for the highway department and their mother, Mary, taught French at St. John's. Mary crocheted a red coat and hat for my Terry Lee doll. I still have it. We all mourned when the Jeffords moved to Orangeburg. For many years, the lots behind our house were vacant, eventually growing up in pine trees and broom straw. This was a playground for us. The boys all seemed to have foxhole shovels, maybe from Cub Scouts; and we were always digging holes, constructing tunnels, and building forts. We also borrowed clippers that we used to cut broom straw to line our structures with or make "brooms." Billy once borrowed Daddy's big clippers and accidently cut Coke's thumb very badly. We rushed Coke home where he fainted from all the blood. It was just one of many trips to the doctor for stitches for most of us. We dug one large tunnel, U-shaped, which was sufficiently long to be dark; so we melted a candle in a tuna can and put it in a small alcove in the middle. Once again, quite unreasonably, the grown-ups made us fill it in for fear one of the smaller children would suffocate in there.

We were not in the city limits, so there was no trash pickup, and a lot of families burned their trash in barrels. These fires occasionally got away, especially in the spring when it was dry, and the broom straw would catch fire. All the neighbors would then try to put the fire out with garden hoses and brooms, so we did not have to call the fire department. I think you had to pay something if you called the fire department. Of course, occasionally, it was one of the children playing with matches. We had rather elaborate war games, hidden forts, etc. in the woods behind where the Pate's house was eventually built. We dug out a bunker, covered it with branches, and then covered all that with pine straw. It was our hideout from the dreaded children from the Other Street. We had no idea that any grown-ups ever went there; and we were horrified when Mrs. Kirven went to rake up pine straw there for her roses, walked on it, and broke her leg. It was well-camouflaged. All of us liked Mrs. Kirven, who was one of the few older people on the street, and we were sorry.

3

The street gradually filled in. The Trulucks and the Welches were welcome additions to our games. The Wall girls moved into the Jeffords' house. Different families moved in and out. We all played football games, the girls usually as cheerleaders or majorettes, mostly in the Sansburys' front yard, or the Browns'. I was thrilled to win a light-up baton in a Hula-Hoop contest at the recreation department. We were very, very good at Hula-Hooping on Greenway Drive. Bike riding and racing were big. Ingram Truluck tells wonderful stories about some of that. We had Southern 500 parades and races, and beauty contests for Miss Greenway Drive as part of our Labor Day celebration. Of course, Labor Day wasn't celebrated in the South. We were really celebrating the races. We had our own Olympics too. The pole vault using a tobacco stake borrowed from Daddy's garden was an excellent way to get splinters. We had the broad jump and races, but the event I remember most was walking the top rail of the Bonnoitts' fence.

Greenway 500 beauty contestants.

And the winner is…Barbara Truluck!

Ingram was big on snakes, and the boys went on snake hunts. Mama always marveled that Dot Truluck, who always looked beautiful and had a white sofa, let Ingram keep snakes in the house. I once saw Dot kill a copperhead in the middle of the street in front of their house. We all knew which ones were poisonous. Some of the older boys on Spring Street and the Other Street were what we knew, even then, to be bullies. They came to sad ends, but one older boy we all loved was our protector. Leonard Ballard was a great guy, who was kind to all of us. He actually lived on Spring Street. I was a skinny thing then, and I still remember in the Browns' front yard, one of the older bullies pushing Billy off his bike, and I just flew at him like a little wet hen. Billy and I fought with each other, but nobody else was going to hurt one of us without the other coming to their defense, and it didn't matter whether it was an adult or a teenager.

Linda, Sandra, Cyndie Wall, and I spent a lot of time playing hopscotch, mostly airplane. We valued colored pieces of glass! It was a life of skinned knees, splinters, stumped toes, and the dreaded sandspurs! We tried to roller skate on the rocky pavement with the skates that were attached with a key to our shoes. We also popped tar bubbles in the summer and got tar on our hot feet. As we got older, we got more daring, sliding down the Spooky Barn metal roof and landing on a pile of pine straw under the eaves. I tore my best wool Bermuda shorts on that roof, and I'm pretty sure someone broke his arm there. Bob Kilgo built a lovely house near that site later. We also had an excellent fort there, with plenty of pine cone ammunition. No one had a TV, and there was nothing to watch most of the time except the test pattern if you did have one. I can't remember when the first TVs arrived on the street, but I do remember watching *The Edge of Night* with the diagonal dark crossing the screen with Robbie at the Browns'. I was not allowed to watch that at my house. We finally got a TV when I was seven.

We spent a good bit of time picking wild plums, an excellent way to get chiggers! I am more careful now when I pick wild plums to make jelly. We had a big grapevine in our side yard, both the purple James grapes and scuppernongs; and all of us picked and ate them. In the fall, the yellow jackets liked them, too, and our bare feet felt the sting. The girls liked to make clover chains, and we sometimes made clothes out of toothpicks and leaves. We had a big gumball tree in our backyard that we loved to climb. If the wind was blowing, we sometimes tied sheets to the branches to make a sail for our tree ship. One early fall when a hurricane was predicted, Billy and I thought this would be our chance to fly if we could just get our pillowcase parachutes airborne. It was six o'clock in the morning. Noni Bonnoitt called my mother and said, "Mary Jane, did you know your children were jumping off your garage roof in their pajamas?" Mama and Daddy had been sound asleep. I was in my pink shorty pajamas. All the girls had shorty pajamas. We did not become airborne. If we had just had a little more wind...

Every so often, the Bonnoitts' grandparents, BooBoo and Pop, would invite us to their farm. They would pick us up on a flatbed truck. They must have had a dairy farm, because we were always given fresh milk. All the men were usually away at work. It was a child-and-woman's world. On a fairly regular basis, there would be a rumor, a whisper of sudden terror, that a mad dog was loose in the area. The word would go out, and all the children were gathered inside to wait until the sheriff came to shoot the dog. Elester, our help, would close the doors and the windows. These were usually strays, not dogs that belonged to the neighborhood.

We loved snow! The best year for snow was in 1960. It snowed every Thursday and Friday for three weeks in a row. We shaved off the tips of two boards we found in the garage and nailed upholstery tape across them to slide our feet into. This worked to a certain degree, but skiing with them was pretty treacherous. We took off the back of a little rocking chair and used the seat and the runners for a sled. This was also pretty treacherous. The remnant of a snowman was still in our front yard at Easter that year.

My parents were big bridge players. They played regularly with the Sansburys, the Jim Browns, the David Browns, and the Smyres. Daddy was still playing with Paul Salisbury and some of the men with connections to the neighborhood when he was in his eighties. As we got older, we drifted into other orbs, and the younger children took over the street life of Greenway Drive; but for the first of us, there was always someone to play with, to look for wildlife prints in the mud with, to search for petrified wood pieces in the little stream, or to have a refreshing chew of sour weed. We could make house plans by raking leaves, admiring the next new baby, eating a half a lemon with sugar on it, or playing house with our dolls. I was so in awe of the Wall girls' Japanese dolls. Remembering them, I bought one for my granddaughter when I went to Japan a year or so ago.

I think our neighborhood had more children than anywhere else in Darlington at the time. There was no organized anything. The minute the workmen left, the new homes under construction were our jungle gyms, the scraps of wood became our fairy tables, the bottle caps their bowls, the sawdust their porridge. It is a wonder we lived through it! I went to Randolph Macon in Virginia, graduated from South Carolina, and lived in Charleston and Columbia before moving to Cheraw, my lawyer husband's hometown. We have two daughters, Sarah and Calder, and two grandchildren. Billy went to South Carolina and MUSC. He is an ophthalmologist in Columbia, has a son Will and daughter Mary, and has three grandchildren. He has operated on a number of our old neighbors. I am not sure that our friends could have imagined that! My mother died in 1970. Daddy continued to live on Spring Street until his death in 1993.

Keith Carter

Born on Greenway Drive

W ho else among us can say they were born on Greenway Drive? Even in 1950, being born at home was unusual, but it happened to me, and it was planned. Here is my story.

My parents moved into a brand-new house on Greenway Drive in 1948, when my brother, Philip, was one year old. It was the third house on the right (it's gone now), coming from Spring Street. About the same time, Richard and Dot Johnson bought and moved in next door, on the Spring Street side. Early in 1950, both my mother and Dot found themselves expecting, with almost identical due dates in early September. Dot was the head nurse at Dr. Coleman's clinic on Cashua Street in town, and she and my mother were good friends. Dot told my mother that there was no reason at all that they shouldn't both have their babies at home, with Dr. Coleman attending. She said there was nothing in an ordinary delivery that couldn't be done at home just as well as at the clinic. She should know, being a registered nurse there. The cost would be less as well, so why not? It was a deal!

The months went by, and not long before the due dates, Dot had some sort of complication that made her decide to have her baby at the clinic after all. My mother stayed with the plan. On September 8, Dr. Coleman was called out to our house, and I was born without any problems. Six days later, Dot had a baby girl at the clinic and named her Susan.

The very first Southern 500 race was held on Labor Day, September 4, 1950 (and my dad told me not too many years ago that he was at that race—I'm not sure that Mom knew). When I became old enough to realize that I was born just four days after that famous Labor Day, I was miffed—the Southern 500 and I were that close to having the same birthday!

Susan Johnson and I lived next door to each other, played in a playpen together, and were strollered on the street together. I'm not sure which year it was, but a few years later, Richard and Dot sold their Greenway house and moved into town, before Susan and I were old enough to actually remember our togetherness time (my mother provided all of this information some years later). Susan and I remained friends and classmates all through school, until that terrible night in December of 1967. In our senior year at St. John's High, she was taken from us in a tragic accident; and I, like everyone else who knew her, was heartbroken. I can definitely say she was my very first friend.

Harvey Drawdy

The Interview

I can vividly remember that beautiful Saturday morning in the summer of 1958, when I left my house in Great Falls, South Carolina, for an appointment with Mr. G. C. Mangum, the superintendent of Darlington Area Schools. I had applied for a teaching position, and this was my first interview. As I drove the one-hundred-mile stretch between Great Falls and Darlington, I could not help but reflect on my life and how I had gotten to this point. Just eight years earlier, I had graduated from Great Falls High School, a wild young buck with no idea what I wanted to do with my life. The Korean War was heating up, so I and some buddies joined the United States Air Force, to avoid being drafted by the Army. I spent the next four years as an MP with "Uncle Sam," touring the world and guarding airplanes, before being stationed at Travis Air Force Base. While at Travis, I married my hometown sweetheart (that's another story in itself), and our first son was born thirteen months later in the base hospital, right before my discharge from the force. We spent that summer at home in Great Falls, waiting for my classes to start at Newberry College. Thanks to the GI Bill, I was going to a four-year college, which seemed impossible just four years earlier. Teaching was never really a priority in my life, but coaching sounded pretty cool, so that's how the Lord worked in my life to get me a degree in teaching. After graduating from college, the Lord had still not convinced me that teaching was my mission in life, but three months in the same old cotton mill that both my parents spent their lives in did.

Now I was being interviewed for a professional teaching job that would turn out to be my "calling" from the Lord. Talk about working in mysterious ways...

As I passed the Darlington Raceway, I wondered if that first car my dad gave me when I finished high school, a 1950 Plymouth, was some kind of omen, because it was the same type of car that won the first race held on the track that I had just passed. My thoughts and reflections seemed to vanish as I pulled into downtown Darlington, and I parked on the square. What a pretty little town, built on a square, just like Winchester, Tennessee, where my maternal grandparents lived and where I spent much of my childhood. Could this be another positive sign from the Lord? As I stood there admiring the town, a very distinguished man walked up and introduced himself as Wade Jordan. He invited me to ride with him, explaining that Mr. Mangum was busy and that it would be a while before I could meet him. Mr. Jordan proceeded to take me on a tour of Darlington and all the local schools. After the tour, he carried me to Mr. Mangum's house on Spain Street. As I stepped out of the car, I was greeted by a large bluetick hound dog. At that moment, I knew this felt like home. Mr. Mangum and I got along great, as we talked about everything from hunting to school business, to salaries, and to expectations for students and teachers. I felt like the interview went well. As we were finishing up, he said to me that he was very impressed, but he never hired a man until he had an opportunity to meet the wife. You see, Mr. Mangum was a very smart man and ahead of his time in that he knew "if Momma ain't happy, nobody is happy," way before it even had become a saying. I told him we would be back the next Saturday, and he said he would have a house for us to look at.

The next Saturday, Merle and I drove to Darlington, met with the Mangums, looked at a small house, and had dinner at a very nice restaurant in Florence. During dinner, he told me that he was very impressed with me but more impressed with Merle, and if we wanted the job, it was ours. We accepted! The house they showed us earlier was available for $40 a month. The night before we were to move, the house we were to move into sold. I called Mr. Mangum, and he said, "Do not worry. Come tomorrow, and I will have you a house to move into." We did and he did. He escorted us to a small house near the end of a street, and that is how the Drawdy family came to reside on Greenway Drive and became lifetime members of the Greenway Drive family. Once a member, always a member!

Fran Wall Weaver

Greenway Drive

L ook Out! It is November 1954; and the Wall family—Frank, Thelma, Cyndie, and Fran—are on the move, landing in Darlington, South Carolina, on glorious Greenway Drive. We had said farewell to friends at the Marine Corps base in Camp Lejeune, North Carolina. Sure, we had plenty of kids to play with on base at Tarawa Terrace. That, however, could not compare with the children in this neck of the woods. This new neighborhood was one like none other. Families adopted us as we shared playdates and birthday parties. Our family rented a small, spiffed-up, cozy white house on Greenway Drive, beside Nancy, Jimmy, Robbie, and Jimbo Brown's home, and facing Evans Circle. This would be our humble abode for at least sixteen months while our daddy, Tech Sergeant Frank Wall, served a tour of duty in Japan assigned as the NCO club manager at South Camp, located at the foot of Mount Fuji.

On the backside of a letter envelope from Daddy, Mother's monthly budget note indicated rent as $50.00, water $3.00, lights $10.00, and milk $3.09. It's a good thing Daddy had great skills playing poker as he supplemented his Marine Corps pay to afford many treats for us, especially for Christmas this year. With Cyndie being six and me two years old, Dad was distraught at not being home with us for the holidays. So he instructed Mother to buy everything for us, asked if she was sure she had enough in his second letter, and in his third note told her to buy more. She followed those instructions. But Mother had a problem. She had not anticipated the skills and tools necessary to assemble our abundant stash of presents. Our loving

Aunt Betty and Uncle Claud Smith always went to Landrum for the Smith family Christmas holiday, so unfortunately, Mama was on her own. Traditionally, on Christmas Eve, a few Greenway Drive dads got together for a celebratory drink after assembling all of their little ones' Santa treats. Two of them became aware of the night-lights burning late across the street in the Wall home. Johnny Bonnoitt and Jimmy Brown (the fathers) came to the rescue. Just like elves, they assembled our Santa treasures. I used to think these men were old, but now that I am old, I realize they were young men just in their early thirties. Cyndie and I will always be thankful for their kind gesture, relieving my mother and saving Christmas Day for two little girls missing their dad. Bimmy (Jimmy Bonnoitt) and I took a ride on the hobby horse his dad had helped assemble. I am not sure where we traveled to.

From left to right: Cynthia, Thelma, Frank, and Fran Wall.

My first memory of my six-foot-one-and-a-half-inch-tall father took place in 1955 when he returned home from his tour of duty in Japan. There in the front yard of our little house on Greenway, he raised me up in his strong, safe arms to a new height. Love Lifted Me. Soon we packed our household goods, left Greenway Drive, and headed to Albany, Georgia, where our dad's new assignment was near Turner Air Force Base. He ran the Base Exchange for the Marine Corps Prepositioned Weapons Depot. Many of us remember sweet, pretty, petite Merle and guitar/harmonica-playing/coon-hunting/ storyteller Harvey Drawdy. Later their family took up residence in the same little house we had rented on glorious Greenway Drive. They brought Stan and Ricky too. What If Walls Could Talk? (By the way, Vera Brasington remembers Harvey's animal pelts hanging on the shed in his backyard).

Stan Drawdy

My Introduction to Greenway Drive

At four years of age, I didn't know too much about the goings-on within my family. My life revolved around watching Captain Kangaroo, eating oatmeal for breakfast, playing outside with my friend, Billy, visiting grandparents, and waiting on Dad to get home from work. I hoped that he would maybe take me fishing, boating, or hunting. We didn't do that stuff every day, but a kid had to be ready just in case Dad said let's go do whatever! Therefore, it came as no surprise that I was completely oblivious to the fact that my dad had taken a job in Darlington, South Carolina, as a seventh-grade science teacher at Brunson-Dargan Jr. High School. Heck, we had just moved from Newberry (where Dad was in college for four years) to Great Falls, South Carolina, where both sets of grandparents lived. Now we were making another move to a dot on the map called Darlington. We had not even been in Great Falls long enough for my grandparents to adequately spoil their only grandchild—ME! But we had been there long enough for Mom to give birth to another son, Ricky. You know, like Ricky Nelson, who was popular back then! He had a cool middle name like "James." Ever heard of James Dean? I was given a cool name too. Stanley, after no one, "duh," and Eugene, after my dad and granddad! At least Eugene rhymes with James Dean—kinda!

This act of naming my brother must have been when Satan introduced me to jealousy! Or maybe it was the fact that this new crying and pooping little brat was taking everybody's time and attention away from ME! I had gone from being corn to only being shucks! And, if that wasn't bad enough, I was beginning to hear words like *Darlington, raceway, nice town, good people*, which led to me learning that we would be leaving Great Falls, my grandparents, and my only friend, Billy. We would be moving a hundred miles away to Darlington, South Carolina, into a new house (ha! It wasn't new!) near the end of the street called Greenway Drive. The words "Greenway Drive" evoked feelings of fear, sorrow, and insecurity. It wasn't long before I found myself stuffed into the backseat of the car surrounded by boxes, suitcases, and clothes, headed for that dot on the map called Darlington. Insecurity and fear ruled the day, especially for me! It was probably the same for Mom. Dad was on an adventure, and Ricky was still crying and pooping. The Drawdys were on their way to Greenway Drive, Darlington, South Carolina!

For some reason, it seemed like the trip took forever. I must have asked, "Are we there yet?" a dozen times, before hearing Dad say, "Almost," just as we were passing by Darlington Raceway. Then, straight into town! The town was built around a square that had a beautiful old building right in the center of it. Dad said, "There is the courthouse!" We drove around the square and turned right onto Cashua Street, then left onto Spring Street. Spring Street was lined with beautiful old huge houses and giant oak trees. We passed Williamson Park, then over Swift Creek bridge, and then turned left onto Greenway Drive! It was like going on an "old town trolley" tour bus as Dad was pointing out all the sights! As we drove down the street to the small house near the end of Greenway Drive, Dad continued the tour, saying, "The high school principal lives there, and a lawyer there, and the football coach in that house." Then he stopped in front of a big, long grassy yard that went from the road a hundred yards back to a small white house facing the street. Dad said, "There she is, HOME SWEET HOME!" The look on Mom's face was definitely not buying what Dad was selling. Unlike me, she had seen the house before when the two of them had gone house-hunting. But I guess houses look different when you are just hunting than they do when you are getting ready to move in.

There were some good points. It had two front doors and two small front porches that looked like two small houses joined together. You could look all the way under the house into the backyard, which I thought was cool! It had a pond behind it! It had a huge front yard for playing football! And you could hear kids playing in the neighborhood so that was a plus to have friends to play with. But the house was not "all that." Dad said it would be great once Mom put her touch on it. Mom said, "Yeah, it would be like polishing a turd!" Anyway, there she was—HOME SWEET HOME! And there we were on Greenway Drive. Little did we know that Greenway Drive and the years spent there with the people, the places, and events would turn out to be the adventure of a lifetime and one of the greatest blessings a family could have!

Mitch Mims

A Special Year

My family moved into a small rental house on Greenway Drive while our house was being built. This was the summer before I started the seventh grade. Let me set the stage by telling where we lived my entire six years of elementary school. The address was Player Street. I was the only boy on that street. There were girls everywhere—even the kids who came to visit other kids were girls. They say timing is everything; and looking back, it would have been fine to live on Player Street with all girls while in high school, or even junior high, but not if you are in elementary school. Being the only boy on the street during those years…pretty much "sucked."

Luckily, I was able to venture out away from Player Street and find a few guys nearby to hang out with. One of those guys was Andy Welch. We soon became best friends. Finally meeting some guy friends and being able to play ball, wrestle, and even fight prepared me just a little bit for my year on Greenway Drive. Soon we made the move, and once we settled into the rental house, I began to feel homesick for Player Street, Andy, my guy friends, and even all the girls. So one morning, I decided to stop moping around. I set out on my bicycle to explore and to "mark my territory" in this new neighborhood. What I saw as I rode from the end of Greenway Drive to the beginning of the street was very exciting to me. I saw basketball goals in many yards, kids playing baseball with plastic balls and bats. I saw footballs and helmets lying on the ground in one yard. Kids were out and about, and most of them were boys. I felt like Dorothy must have felt going from Kansas in black-and-white to all the colors and excitement of munchkin land—so much to see and to discover!

What I discovered on my bike that day was better than anything in any candy store. This was the beginning of one of the best years of my childhood. Riding back and forth and up and down the street that morning, I remember seeing two kids playing in the front of their house. They looked like they could be brothers. I could tell they were watching me and talking about me, so I looked over that way. When I did, the older kid motioned for me to come into the yard. He introduced himself as Stan and told me that the other kid was his little brother, Ricky. Then he welcomed me to Greenway Drive. We started playing, and soon the parents came out of the house to meet the new kid. That's when I felt this would be a special place to live. Turns out that this was the beginning of a lifelong (sixty years and still going) friendship with the Drawdy family.

Let me lay out Greenway Drive as I remember it through the eyes of a ten-year-old kid. As you turn off Spring Street onto Greenway Drive, Stan and Ricky lived in the fifth house on the right. Two houses down on the right were the Howle brothers, Wayne and Ken. Lots of good golf and basketball came out of that home, and two more great friends for me. The next house was Brent Sansbury, another successful businessman, now somewhere in the upstate of South Carolina. Around the curve past the apartments lived Pete and Jeff Sansbury. Both were fun to hang out with as kids. Both were good football players. Last I heard, Pete is living out west and is a big-time psychologist or something like that. Jeff is still in Darlington. We rented the house next to Pete and Jeff, so I saw them daily while living on the Drive. Go to the end of the street, around Dewitt Circle, and when you get back to the big curve, look to the right, and that is where the Trulucks lived. Ingram is a bit older than me, and we became friends much later in life, but his younger brother, Johnny, was closer to my age, and we became friends too. Johnny was a very gifted athlete in both football and track. He was one of the fastest kids in town. I can still remember that #20 breaking off long touchdown runs for the Blue Devils. Our Lord took Johnny home as a very young man. I guess God needed a good guy and a great running back in heaven.

Then you pass Coach Welch's house, and you are at Andy and Danny Sansbury's house. They were both very smart and easy to be friends with. Next up was Johnny and Jimmy Bonnoitt, better known as Punk and Bimmy. Now I should disclose that I became good friends with both of them and still am today. They both still work and live in Darlington. But they both had a mean streak when they were younger. You certainly did not want to cross either of them. They were good athletes also and played football and track for the Blue Devils. They lived right across the street from Stan and Ricky, and sometimes they would come over to play. When you played with them, they were in charge for sure, and usually someone would be tied to a tree or locked up in one of Harvey Drawdy's dog pens. We rarely ever saw them together at the same time, but when we did, it was good because they usually wound up fighting each other rather than picking on us. We often played at the Drawdy house under those big oak trees, and we played marbles a lot. One day, we had a big marble fest going on. A bunch of kids were there with their marbles…and we always played for keeps. That meant if you won you got to keep the other kid's marbles. It wasn't long before the fest was over. Punk and Bimmy had done taken all the marbles on Greenway Drive. That ended marble playing for a few days, and then the Bonnoitt brothers gave all the marbles back so we could play some more. It was a great time.

Looking back, I realize that in that one year I made a lifetime of friends. They took me in as if I had always been there. Even today, my Greenway Drive network is strong and supportive. I thank God for giving me that special year and all my special friends. And to all my Greenway Drive friends, thank you for making that one year special for me and my family, and for all your support over the years. And always remember this: "Once a Greenway Driver, always a Greenway Driver!"

Ingram Truluck

The Greenway Drive
Southern 500

I discovered NASCAR racing on Labor Day 1955. Dad was attending the Southern 500, and Mom was listening to the radio broadcast of the race. She was very excited about the victory of Herb Thomas. It was Chevrolet's first visit to the famed Darlington Victory Lane. Back then the Ford and Chevrolet rivalry was as intense as that of the New York Yankees and the Brooklyn Dodgers. Victory meant a year of bragging and lying. Defeat meant a year of excuses and lying. There was also a fierce loyalty to Pontiac, Oldsmobile, Chrysler, Dodge, Mercury, Buick, DeSoto, Plymouth, and the "Fabulous Hudson Hornet." We children were mesmerized by racing, and many of us transformed into real race car drivers in the magical neighborhood of Greenway Drive in Darlington. Our bicycles became stock cars, and "the Greenway Drive Southern 500" was born. Our tracks were Greenway Drive, Dewitt Raceway, Kilgo Raceway, and Smyre Raceway. Our first superspeedway course included Greenway Drive, Evans Circle, and part of Spring Street, clockwise. However, riding bikes up the Spring Street hill, in front of the Cains' house, was too exhausting. After just a few laps we were out of breath, enthusiasm, and IQ. It was a dark day for the stockholders.

The second Greenway Drive Raceway was created and became our favorite because we could race on pavement from the third and fourth turns through the front stretch. The first and second turns were not on pavement, and we had a real guardrail which was Howard

Sansbury's white wooden fence. The back stretch was flanked by the "Spooky Barn," which is still standing and remains the home of several monsters. The Greenway Drive home stretch was in front of the Truluck home, coincidentally. This racetrack was very difficult to improve on, but we did try others. The Smyres' new home off Medford was the first in that neck of the woods and was very isolated. Getting there felt like walking to Wyoming. We tried establishing a track there, but it didn't catch on.

Leonard Ballard was our leader. He taught us about the Bible, racing, building forts, exploring, pine cone battles, animals, and living out our imaginations. We called him "Leo." Leo was a blend of Billy Graham, John Wayne, Jimmy Stewart, Eddie Albert, and Fireball Roberts. We were a challenge for him, with our intellectual indexes below sea level and our grammar skills anemic. Long, drawn-out, disconnected Southern sentences would bring out a well-deserved "Stooo-PID" from Leo. If things were really going badly, we could be addressed as "IDJITS." That was even lower than "idiots."

Racing fever was unleashed and proliferated. There was no cure in sight. When we began practicing and qualifying, we realized a major ingredient in the thrill of racing was missing. There was no dramatic sound of race car engines coming from our bicycles. Our first "popper" shop was opened, and for a price, a custom piece of cardboard would be attached by a clothespin near the spokes. This gave us the sound we needed. Our car loyalty was influenced by what our parents owned. If your parents owned a Chevy, then you could be Speedy Thompson in the number 46 Chevrolet. A Ford could be Curtis Turner in Number 26. Here's an example of how real this was to us; one summer, Leo was consistently fastest in practice and qualified as Cotton Owens in the number 6 Pontiac. Because of Leo's success in a Pontiac, a few of us discussed and considered switching to Pontiacs!

I forgot to mention that for a while we called the poppers "mufflers." Somehow, we thought mufflers made noise. We must have stayed home from school the day mufflers were discussed.

We could barely sleep the night before race day. It was the grand crescendo following weeks of practice and qualifying, with a real parade down Greenway Drive and a Miss Greenway Drive Southern 500 beauty pageant. The street was blocked off, and this meant no traffic past Coach Welch's house.

For years, "Dixie" was played during the parade and pace laps at Darlington Raceway, along with the announcer Ray Melton's "Gentlemen, start your engines!" There was enough electricity in the air to launch chill bumps out of your spine into orbit. Leo decided it was imperative that we have "Dixie" during our parade and pace laps, so he led all of us drivers in the singing of "Dixie" as we passed in review in front of the neighborhood fans! What a blessing those times were.

From back row, left to right: Robert Payne, Leonard
Ballard, Ingram Truluck, and Philip Carter.
From second row: Keith Carter, Johnny "Punk" Bonnoitt,
Johnny Truluck, and Jimmy "Bimmy" Bonnoitt (hidden).
From front row: Billy Cain with a clipboard
and Tommy Wilson with a flag.

As Paul Harvey used to say, "Let's take an over-the-shoulder backward glance," a glance to Labor Day 1950. Make no mistake about it, Darlington put NASCAR on the map and into the Big Time. It wasn't the other way around; and it wasn't Daytona, Charlotte, or Atlanta that did it. Those tracks were built years after Darlington had paved the way and set the standard. It would have been fitting if Harold Brasington had waved the green flag for the first Southern 500, but he didn't have to. Harold Brasington WAS the green flag! He did the impossible, and Darlington is one of the most well-known towns in the world.

Sometime later, a few of us kids were in the Cains' yard, looking down on Spring Street. Leo waved as he walked by, headed uptown. He was going to meet with his friends and was wearing an alpaca sweater, Weejuns, and Gold Cup socks. Leo was now a teenager, and we all knew that a big part of our Greenway Drive was gone with the wind. That was the very day that our bicycles miraculously changed from race cars back into ordinary bikes. The sun of our childhood may have been heading for the horizon, but it hadn't set for us yet. We were, and still are, very thankful for the amazing times!

Merle Drawdy

The Glue

Lottie Bryant and I would often talk and make plans for the weekend. Our goal was to get our guys to take us out on Saturday nights. Once Lottie came up with a plan for us to work hard and get all our chores done early…the laundry, the housework, children fed, then we could dress up; and maybe…just maybe, our husbands would get the message and take us out on the town. After all, we deserved it! We both worked during the week and still found time to keep the house up, cook the meals, and tend to the children. Now our men were more of the outdoor types. On Saturdays, they would be out hunting or fishing, whatever season was in, and when they would get in from the outing, they would head straight to Harvey's shop and start cleaning whatever game they had caught or killed that day. Before Lottie and I could even get noticed by those guys, they would have the outdoor cooker going, frying up fish or making a squirrel stew. I do not think either one of our husbands ever noticed that we had gotten dressed to go out. Lottie and I would just look at each other and shake our heads. We didn't know what to think, much less what to say. I don't remember if we ever got our night out on the town with our guys. Seemed like a night out was a pipe dream for us. Like the song says, "Now and then there's a fool such as I." After several attempts at getting the guys' attention, it seemed futile and even foolish. But we still were looking for some time to have fun.

We didn't give up. We were bound and determined to have some fun, so we decided to forget the guys and plan a ladies' night out. What could we do without the menfolk? Then it hit us…cards.

Some of the girls in the neighborhood knew how to play bridge and canasta, and even had clubs that met once a week. At that time, I had only played old maids, Go Fish, and Crazy Eights. I was dumb as dirt when it came to high-class card games, but Lottie and I were bound and determined to learn how to play good enough to be invited to a bridge and canasta club night or better yet to start our own club. That was it…start our own club one night a week, alternate houses, time with good friends, drinking coffee, smoking Virginia Slims, catching up on the local gossip. How could it get much better than that?

Well! Easier said than done. Who would have thought it would be hard to find four ladies to fill the card table? We had me, Lottie, Margie Lynch, and then played the dickens trying to find that fourth person each week. Sherrill McKelvey would sometimes play and Dot Sansbury, or Tootsie Howle sometimes; and sometimes it would just be three of us there. Desperate times lead to desperate measures…so occasionally, Sherrill's husband, Jimmy, would fill in as our fourth member for ladies' night. But that wasn't the worst of it. Before we could go play, we had to cook supper, feed the kids, clean the kitchen, and hardest of all…coax our husbands into allowing us the night off. Seriously…girls' night out was not the norm in those days. But the good thing was that we always had fun. And we looked forward to our fun times together.

When I look back at how much fun it was, I realize how much we needed that time. This was during the time when our kids were young. We worked outside the home in addition to all the household chores. "A woman's work is never done." No truer statement has ever been said. That little bit of free and fun time renewed us for the week. Life was good but could be hard too.

When we moved away from Greenway Drive, I lost track and lost contact with most of those ladies. Greenway Drive was blessed with many kids and lots of great men. But the strength of our neighborhood, and the "glue" that held families together, was the wives and moms of Greenway Drive.

Keith Carter

Growing Up on Greenway Drive Part 1

In 1948, my parents bought a small new house, one of about a half dozen in a row that were built by Paul Psillos, on the right as you turned onto Greenway Drive from Spring Street. Greenway was a dead-end street which became a true baby boom neighborhood with the influx of many young families that were eager to return to civilian life after World War II. My birth year, 1950, may have been the peak year for babies born in our neighborhood. Besides me, there was Susan Johnson, Barbara Truluck, David Brown and Jimmy (Jimbo) Brown (first cousins), Robin Mills, Dane Smyre, and Chafee Jones (who lived just across Spring Street)—all born in 1950.

I like to think about growing up on Greenway Drive. I will always be grateful that it is where my parents chose to live as they started their family. I tell people it is thanks to Adolf Hitler that I was ever born (along with my brother and sister). We are in no way unique, as World War II changed the course of millions of lives in America and around the world. My father, Donald, was born and raised on a farm in the Rio Grande Valley of Texas, just sixteen miles from the border with Mexico. It is doubtful he would have ever known anyone in South Carolina had it not been for Mr. Hitler and the war he created. He was drafted at eighteen and was trained as a medic in the US Army, then stationed on a hospital ship. The ship was bound for France to pick up the war-wounded after D-Day in

1944, but the ship was old and had to stop by the Charleston Navy Yard for repairs before crossing the Atlantic. My mother was a 1941 graduate of Bishopville (South Carolina) High School and, along with a female cousin or two, had gone to the Charleston Navy Yard to seek clerical work, which they found. It was there that my Texan father and South Carolinian mother met, fell in love, and married as soon as the war was over and he was discharged from the Army. They decided to live in South Carolina, and he went to work for the JR Watkins Products Co., which assigned him to the Florence-Darlington District. Of all the places they could have chosen to buy a home, they chose Greenway Drive!

Rumor had it that at one time, Greenway Drive was just a dirt lane to the horse stable and a horse track that were at the end of the street. The stable became known to all the kids on Greenway Drive as the Spooky Barn, and the property was owned by the Kilgo family, who didn't live there until the late '50s when they built a new home on the property. This is where Bobby (one year older than me) and Evalyn (one year younger) lived. The horses and other vestiges of the past, except the Spooky Barn, were long gone by the time the baby boom arrived.

We were fascinated by the Spooky Barn and played all around it, treating it like a neighborhood park facility that belonged to all of us. The main thing we did at the Spooky Barn was slide down the tin roof. We would take a handful of pine straw with us to the peak of the roof, sit on it to eliminate the friction, and slide down onto an almost flat shed roof that extended out at one section. We did this over and over until we became tired of it. One hazard of sliding on the tin roof was that some of the nails protruded a bit, and sometimes we would catch our pants on a nail head. This happened to me once, and my pants and underwear were ripped, exposing one butt cheek. I was not hurt, but I was mortified that I had to walk all the way down the street to get home, deathly afraid some girl might see me. When I passed a house where a girl lived, I walked sideways, holding the rip together with my hand; I'm sure that was very inconspicuous. I was about five years old at the time.

Front: Keith Carter, Barbara Truluck, Ingram Truluck, and Philip Carter.
Back: Maria and Eddie Young.

One notable day in my early life, a pipeline was being installed on Greenway, requiring a narrow ditch to be dug alongside the street. I was curious about the work and went out to investigate, and the workmen were all looking at a layer of seashells that had been discovered a couple of feet down. The talk was about how the ocean had obviously once covered our part of the state, and I'll never forget that.

Another thing that I vividly remember is the human skull that was in the yard where Bobby Truluck lived, on the corner of Pinehaven and Spring Street. Bobby told us that his uncle brought it home from the war and that it was a Japanese skull. I remember picking it up and examining it then dropping it back to the ground and moving on. We thought little of it since it was common to us, thinking that every neighborhood probably had at least one human skull lying around. A number of our neighbors' houses had a large brass cannon shell casing, brought back from the war, standing just inside the front door, put to good use holding umbrellas. Many of the dads had a small folding Army-issued shovel that was used to dig foxholes, which we put to similar use. And many homes had the prickly brown Army blankets that the dads also brought home from the war. We played Army in the yard and woods beside Jim Brown's house; half were GIs, and the other half were Japs. We fired imaginary machine guns at each other. *Eh-eh-eh-eh-eh-eh-eh* was our stuttering machine-gun sound, and we lobbed pine cone hand grenades at each other. "You're dead!" "No, I'm not!" Such were the reminders of the horrendous war that most of our dads had participated in. We were quite unaware of the tragedy and loss that the war had cost our country and the world; all we knew was that our dads were in it and were fine. That's the merciful innocence of youth.

Bicycles were our vehicles on Greenway Drive. All were single-speed models—no gears—with fat tires and no hand brakes. Bikes with gears, hand brakes, and skinny tires were called "English bikes," and they were mostly a myth to us. After I got my first bicycle, I seldom walked anywhere. My brother, Philip, and I both got bikes for Christmas in 1956. His was a new twenty-four-inch JC Higgins model (from Sears Roebuck) with all the trimmings, while mine was a very plain little twenty-inch model, which I was very happy with. My little bike served me well for many years, and it was after we moved to McIver Road that I got a larger one which had belonged to Butch Welch of Greenway Drive! My mother saw it for sale in the *News and Press*, inquired, and found she was talking to Belva Welch. Butch had used it on his paper route—a blue twenty-six-inch Schwinn with a large basket. I loved that bike and put many miles on it!

We also roller-skated on the street in those years (no sidewalks to be found). Our skates were the clamp-on type which required a key to tighten, had leather straps that buckled around the ankles, and could be used only with leather oxford shoes. Before I learned to really crank down the key, I had some near wipeouts when a skate would come loose at the front and dangle disastrously—always when I was really speeding. One vivid memory is the time Philip and I decided to go to Parnell's Store on N. Main Street. He may have been ten at the time, and I would have been seven. This trip required us to go to the Dewitts' house at the end of Greenway Drive, cross the dam behind their house, and come out at the Rabbs' house on N. Main or maybe the Muldrows'. From that point on, we had a luxurious sidewalk down the hill to skate on, all the way to Parnell's Store. But there was this one big oak tree which had a semicircular jut-out in the brick wall, which the sidewalk went around; not being able to slow down one bit, I slammed into it and split my lips pretty good. Philip had on a red shirt, and he got me to blot my lips on his sleeve since it wouldn't show the blood. That was a good brother! We went on to the store, and I suppose we bought something, but the mood was spoiled for me. We trudged back up the hill and back home. I can assure you our mother didn't know anything about this escapade, and except for the split lip, we did just fine.

On Greenway Drive, the boys were known for two main activities: racing things and catching snakes. For both of these pastimes, I can thank our ringleader, Ingram Truluck, who had a passion for both. We raced bicycles and model cars on the street, and little boats in the creek. We cut cardboard flaps from the many Watkins boxes my dad discarded and fastened them on our bikes with clothespins to make our bikes sound like race cars. We WERE Fireball Roberts, Curtis Turner, Speedy Thompson, and Buck Baker. Our bicycles WERE Chevrolets, Fords, Pontiacs, and Mercurys (nobody wanted to drive a Nash). We hung cardboard placards with our car numbers from the crossbar of our bicycles, which corresponded to the real number of the driver we became. The biggest bike race ever staged while we lived on Greenway, and it must have been in 1957, was the race that began across from Ingram's house, went down Greenway for a bit, then turned left and went between the woods and the Sansburys' fence to the Kilgos' lane, turned left again and went by the Spooky Barn and the Mills' house, to the street and left again, and went around the curve and back to the start-finish line to complete a lap. (There were no houses then between the Sansburys' and the Mills' houses—only woods). At the first ninety-degree turn in the woods, we piled cardboard boxes from my father's business (since we didn't have any hay bales) to supposedly cushion the crash if somebody missed the turn. I found out that cardboard boxes are not very cushiony. To make it more realistic, as well as to involve girls in the event, there were nurse volunteers on hand in case of accidents, and several were positioned at the cardboard box suicide corner.

I devised a plan to accidentally-on-purpose crash into the boxes after about five laps, knowing I had no chance of competing with the older boys in the race. This took care of a couple of things at once: my race would be honorably over, and I would be attended to by the pretty nurses. Once the race got underway and I started getting tired, my handlebars got abnormally wobbly as I approached the corner, and I made sure to miss the nurses. Then…*whammo-bammo*! I was into the box barrier with only elbows and rear end showing! It worked out perfectly, except I got pretty dinged up by the hard corners of the boxes—I didn't even have to fake being hurt. The photo on page 24 indicates there were eight racers and two officials in this notable event.

Stan Drawdy

Dress to Impress

(This story was requested by Mom and is dedicated to all the older brothers out there whose main job in life was, and still is, to torment their younger brother). After living in Dr. Wilson's rental house for three years, my parents bought a house up the street, and we moved. You might say that Ricky and I had a double blessing in that we moved to Greenway Drive twice. Maybe that is why Tami and Tiffni never got to live on Greenway Drive. Rick and I had used up their blessing for it. By the time Tami was born, we had moved away from Greenway Drive, and then Tiff came along four years after Tami.

So we moved to 112 Greenway Drive when I was seven years old and Ricky was only three, so his torment had not really started yet. I don't know much about sibling rivalry or the psychology of birth order, but what I do know is that once Ricky got old enough to play outside with the bigger boys…like me…my freedom as I knew it was over. "Stan, let your brother play." "Stan, watch after Rick…don't let him get hurt." "Stan, let your brother hold the football." They say that success breeds success, and Ricky had learned well what worked in his favor…crying! All he had to do was start his crying routine and call my name out in a crying tone, and I would get "the business," as Wally would say on *Leave It to Beaver*. I would get yelled at, Rick would get what he wanted, and Mom would get a few minutes of peace till the next go-round. Sometimes, as Mom would walk into the house, having handled a crying spell, she would say, "Ricky, if you would just go one whole day without crying, I'll give you $10." I don't think Rick ever collected.

I had lots of friends on Greenway Drive, and there were usually several kids in our yard. We had a great yard for playing. The front yard was great for football and baseball. We had a hedge on one end of the field. We couldn't play football between the hedges as they do in Georgia, but we could play behind the hedges, which was just as good. Also, the hedge served as an outfield fence for knocking home runs when we played Wiffle baseball. The only problem with the hedge was that when the Wiffle ball got stuck in the hedge, as it did often, there were wasp nests built in it, and we often got stung. So that was a good job for the younger brothers.

Our side yard had a big tree, and Dad trimmed some limbs on one side and put my basketball goal up there. It became the best place to play half-court basketball. In the backyard was Dad's workshop, some scrubby-looking ole shrubs, and fences across the back and down the sides. I remember once Mom was telling Dad that they needed to fix up the yard and make it look nice—maybe plant some grass in the front yard and keep the kids off of it for a while…get that yard looking good. Then in the same conversation, they realized that pretty yards could come later; but for now, they were in the business of raising kids, not grass!

Behind our house was Kilgos' woods, great for playing army or cops and robbers. The point is we had lots of different things to play, and we could switch from one game to another without missing a beat. And that's exactly what we did.

You know how kids go through that stage where they want to wear uniforms. One can really get into some serious playing when they dress the part. Girls especially like to play dress-up, and they carry it to the extreme with the makeup and all the princess dresses and mermaid tails, etc. Well, when you think about it, adults like to wear uniforms too. Think about business attire, medical and hospital wear (scrubs), military, law enforcement. Even leisure activities invite a change of clothing…golfers, hunters, riding horses, beach attire, and workout clothing. Part of the human experience is to dress to impress, to dress the part—to have all the gadgets and equipment that go along with whatever activity in which you are involved.

I went through all that to say this…on Greenway Drive, most of us had uniforms and equipment for certain things like recreation leagues, teams we were on, places we went for lessons or instructions, and more. But when engaged in free play, whatever we had on at the time was our pretend uniform for that setting. So most of us could switch from sport to sport, activity to activity instantly. But not my brother Rick! He had to have on the right clothes for the activity of the moment. And he had a great collection to choose from, down to the specific headgear that goes with the uniforms. He had cowboy, army, football, baseball, hunting, cops, and even robbers. If we started to play football, he would run inside and get Mom to find his football uniform and help him get it on, and then he would come running back out to play. Soon my favorite game was to see how many times we could make Ricky change clothes. We would start a game like football. Rick would run in to get Mom to help him get dressed for football, and then he would come back outside ready to play football…all decked out in cleats, socks, football pants, shoulder pads, jersey, and helmet. It would be a good thirty minutes before he would be ready to play. Once he emerged from the house ready to play football, we would change the activity to baseball. We would start playing, and Rick would run home to get his baseball uniform on. Sometimes, we would make him change three or four times before he actually got to play. We thought it was fun, Rick probably thought it was mean, and to Mom…it had to be aggravating.

Ricky finally outgrew the desire to always dress the part, at least to some degree. He became a good athlete like most of us on Greenway Drive. He played football and baseball for the Blue Devils. His career turned out very good as he served the state of South Carolina as a football and baseball coach, athletic director, and math teacher, being an award winner and recognized for his success in each category. I was most proud of my brother when he was inducted into the Darlington High School Hall of Fame…and yes, he was dressed to impress!

Who Knew?

It would not have been unusual in the late 1950s or early 1960s to see us guys on Greenway Drive carrying around a shoebox, as we went from house to house. Most of us were, or should I say could have been, megawealthy at this current time of our lives if only we still had what was in our shoeboxes. For many of us, those shoeboxes held our most prized possessions. Some kids had more than one shoebox full.

Back in those days, kids didn't have much money to carry around; heck, most of our parents didn't even have carry-around money. So we actually developed our own currency with the items in our boxes, and we used it like cash to barter for things other kids might have that we wanted. Our new currency was pretty much useless if you needed to barter with one of the girls in the neighborhood, because it had no value to females. I'm not trying to be politically incorrect or unwoke, but that was just a fact. Girls wanted no part of what guys carried around in their shoeboxes, but for us guys, we traded them back and forth like stocks on the stock market. Little did we know that what we had, in some cases, would be more valuable than many stocks are today. We even found other uses for our "kid currency." Once I saw a kid use some of his currency like kindling to help start a fire. I've seen the currency used like a puzzle and put together end to end and then framed in a picture frame and hung on the wall in a kid's room. And twice a year, we used them to make a loud noise. One of the kids figured out that you could use several units of Kid Currency and several of Mom's wooden clothespins to clip them onto the spokes of your bike, and it made your bike sound like it had a motor. So every year when we had the auto races in Darlington, it seemed quite natural for Greenway Drive to hold bicycle versions of the races on the same day as the auto races, and that's when we used a good amount of our currency to make the bikes sound like they had motors. Baseball cards were just thick enough to make a loud sound but not too thick that they wouldn't stay clipped onto the spokes as you pedaled your way to the finish line of our Rebel 300 and Southern 500 bike races.

We used up a lot of currency during those two races—wasted a lot of baseball cards that would be valuable today, I'm sure. But who knew? Baseball cards were easy to come by back in those days. Every kid was a collector, so none of us ever thought they were worth much…except in our own barter system. Just like traders today, certain cards were worth more. A Mickey Mantle card was worth two Clete Boyer cards and worth a dozen Harry Byrd cards. Topps was the most popular brand of cards. Found in most candy cases at stores, one could get a chunk of bubblegum and a card. Post Toasties cards came on the back of Post cereal boxes. And there were other brands of cards and many gimmicks to get you to buy things by throwing in baseball cards. I remember in 1961 when Mickey Mantle and Roger Maris were battling for the home run title and record, a movie came to Darlington Cinema about them. It wasn't a great movie, more like a documentary, but they were giving away autographed cards by Mickey Mantle and Roger Maris to the first so-many who came to the movie. Several of Greenway Drive kids got there early and waited, and we did get the cards, and those were the "holy grail" of baseball cards at the time.

The best way to improve your collection of cards was to be good at a game we invented called stickball. In stickball, you had to find a sandy place, usually under oak trees or in a driveway, where you could draw out a baseball diamond. Each player would select nine cards to be his team. A small stick was used as the bat; and a marble, usually a solid crystal rather than a cat's-eye, was the ball. As the team manager, you were the pitcher (you rolled the marble toward home plate) and the batter (you swung the stick at the marble as it rolled to you). The team in the field consisted of cards of the players laid out by position. The team batting consisted of the players' cards stacked up, ready to bat one at a time. When your opponent rolled the marble at you, you hit it with the stick. If it rolled over a player card in the field, you were out and the next batter up. If it did not touch a player card of the opponent, you had a hit, and the player card you hit for moved to the bases accordingly. Anything shy of the outfielders was a single, in the gap a double, on the warning track a triple; and if it went beyond the drawn-in fence line, it was a home run. We played nine full innings, and the winner got all of the loser's cards for his own. Sometimes, if both managers owned a full major league team, we would put up a full team against a team. My understanding is that a full team is very valuable. I had several full teams that I had won in my collection. Not only did we have valuable collections of baseball cards and invent a great game that was later marketed by one of the toy makers, but we also invented and mastered a new form of gambling. Winner-take-all!

Those were some great times and lots of fun. After we moved from Greenway Drive, I do not remember ever collecting cards again. I do remember taking my box of cards and storing them away in the closet of my new room at our new house. They stayed there for many years until I graduated from St. Johns and went off to Clemson. While I was at Clemson, Ricky (my brother) took over my room. All my stuff left in the closet got moved into the attic. I never thought of those cards again until my parents' house fire that started in the attic due to a faulty attic fan. Charred and singed pieces of baseball cards were all that was found of my collection during the cleanup. If I had been smart, I would have retrieved my valuable collection from Mom's attic. And if we had been smart, we would have patented the stickball game and packaged it in a rectangular box that looked like a major league stadium.

But WHO KNEW? "Dad-gummit!"

Barbara Welch Haynes

Greenway Drive Memories

My family moved from Spain Street to Greenway Drive in 1955 when I was three years old (you can do the math!). My next-door neighbor, Barbara Truluck, told me later, because I have very few memories of these early days, that she came over to my house several different times to ask my mother, Belva, what her little girl's name was. I guess the name Barbara was hard for her to remember! There were also a few fingerprints in a small retaining wall at the den door that may have been made by a neighborhood child or two—I'm not sure!

Foods

In those days, we had quite the outdoor diet. We chewed on sour weed, wondered if a dog had been by before us; ate wild green plums, we couldn't wait for them to get ripe; crabapples, not good, but maybe they weren't ripe either; and grapes when we could sneak them. We had a wonderful indoor diet too. I don't remember names, but I think we had some jelly makers and maybe a winemaker or two. My daddy, Jim Brown, and Robert Mills grew some delicious tomatoes. My family was fortunate enough to be gifted apricot leather from Bill Cain at Christmas. Boy, I would love a piece of that again. One of our indoor-outdoor staples was popcorn and Kool-Aid. The master chefs of these treats were Mary Ann Sansbury and Thelma Wall. Many days, a pack of us would end up in Mary Ann's backyard playing. I don't know if we looked hungry, if we asked for food, or if she just knew kids were always hungry; but she would make popcorn, and I think pass it out the window to us. We didn't wash our hands before eating; wonder how we survived! Thelma also made a lot of popcorn for us. Sometimes, even popcorn balls—what a sticky mess! One day, some of us girls were on the small side porch of Fran's house. I don't know if it was a special occasion or not, but Thelma was making popcorn for us. We heard some strange noises from the kitchen, and when we went into the house to check it out, we saw that Thelma had forgotten to put the lid on the popcorn pot, and popcorn was popping all over the kitchen! Oh, what a hoot. We all laughed, even Thelma!

Spooky Barn

Many towns have haunted houses or trails or strange happenings in a graveyard. But Greenway Drive had something much better. We had the Spooky Barn. I don't know why it was called that; maybe I was the only one who did. But it was so cool! I believe the Boy Scouts met in one of the rooms. It seems like the room was always locked, but I do remember going into it one time. It must have been left unlocked because we would NEVER break in! To me, the best thing about the Spooky Barn was climbing up on the roof. You see, the roof was tin, and it made the best slide ever. You just had to be sure your clothes or any part of your person did not get caught on any nails. And you had to know how to slow yourself down when you got to the bottom. If you didn't, you would probably slide right off to a ten-foot drop, ouch! If you sat on the peak of that tin roof, you could see into the neighborhood. We played many games using the basketball goal that was nailed to the side of the barn. HORSE was a favorite. One had to be careful when attempting a layup. The barn wall was very hard!

Games

Growing up on Greenway Drive, we always had indoor-outdoor activities we played. No iPhone or tablet games for us. Vera and I played many games of War, using cards, of course. We played Red Rover, Mother May I (always using our manners or you lost your turn), and Ain't No Boogers Out Tonight (but not correct grammar). A lot of these games took place in the Trulucks' and Sansburys' yards. Then there were the games that took place all over the neighborhood. We would pick teams and play cops and robbers or just have a good old-fashioned pine cone war. It's amazing; I don't think anyone got seriously hurt during these games. However, Punk found out that it wasn't so easy to "rack up" (tackle) a girl when playing football! We rode bikes, sometimes all day long. When I first started riding, I could not go past the creek; then I was promoted to Evans Circle, then finally graduated to Spring Street. We were outside riding bikes sometimes all day long. I was riding with Fran and Vera, three across the road, when Jimmy Brown's bird dog named Francis decided to cross the road. I have no memory of this accident or what happened earlier in the day. I was told that Francis missed Fran and Vera, and I ran smack-dab over her and landed on the pavement, hitting my head. I was told Fran and Vera had a serious discussion!

Jim Brown

The Greenway Drive 300

The year was 1960. All the kids in the neighborhood could hear the distant moan of the stock cars as they cranked up for time trials a week before the Rebel 300. Racing season had begun in Darlington, and it was time to get our cars ready. No, not full-size, grown-up cars like the ones piloted by Junior Johnson and Buck Baker but scale-model Fords, Chevrolets, and Plymouths that we had purchased from Winnie, the gracious lady behind the counter of Farmer's Hardware. She made sure she had the newest models from Detroit, ten-inch-long plastic reproductions with metal undercarriages. After making our selections, we would rush home and begin modifications, starting with ripping off the hollow plastic wheels and replacing them with soft rubber tires scavenged from toys sold by Rose's Five and Ten. Next, we unscrewed the body of our cars from the frame and removed the seats. This allowed us the space to tape two D-size flashlight batteries to the undercarriage. The batteries gave the car added weight. After reattaching the body, we would decorate the hood and sides with decals left over from glue-together model kits. We would swap decals with friends—two STPs for a Pure Oil or one Hooker Headers for a Goodyear and a Champion Spark Plugs. Then we would paint the number of our favorite driver on the roof. I was #22, Fireball Roberts. Fireball had an "Aw Shucks" outward demeanor that, combined with flat-out pedal-to-the-metal driving skills, made him a hero in my ten-year-old eyes. Was there ever anything cooler than the sight of Fireball leaning against the door of his 1957 Chevy? He was the Mickey Mantle and the Johnny

Unitas of NASCAR, all rolled into one. In 1958, Fireball won the Darlington Southern 500, as well as races at Atlanta International and Daytona. By 1960, he had switched to driving a Pontiac, and my model racer was soon decaled up and ready to go.

We would hold our race on a Saturday near the real race day. The major organizers of our event were Leonard and Ingram. Leonard was the grand instigator, and Ingram was the master of ceremonies. Being older, they also both had hellacious cars. A few rungs below them in the neighborhood pecking order were myself, David, Dane, and Keith; in later years, younger kids would join the driver's ranks. On race day morning, a white starting line was painted on the road. For each lap, a "driver" would place his heels behind the line, bend over, and propel his car between his legs. Each driver took turns, and the car that went the furthest distance before coming to a stop would win that lap. The car with the most winning laps would win the race. Sounds simple, but pushing the car could be a delicate operation. You wanted to use a lot of force, but too much muscle could cause the car to spin out or even flip over. A long, smooth ride was desired. As the race wore on, the car might need adjustments, and you were allowed a pit stop, but your chance of winning that lap was gone. Occasionally, a car would rocket along the asphalt and crash into another car that was on the track, an event that would result in angry shouts, accusations, and threats (just like real racing!). After a designated number of laps, a winner would be declared. Afterward, we would sit in the shade of the big sycamore tree in my front yard, drink ice-cold orange TruAdes, and eat Nabs and Banana Flips. And the prize for all this effort? To tell the truth, I can't remember what the winner got. But it really didn't make any difference. We were racing. Afterword: Fireball Roberts died in 1964, from complications that resulted from a crash at Charlotte Motor Speedway.

Harvey Drawdy

The Children of Greenway Drive

O n my first trip to Darlington and to Greenway Drive, I was impressed with the number of kids I saw out playing that day. I was impressed because I knew it had to be a good place for raising kids. Sixty-three years later, I am still impressed with the young people who grew up there and the adults that they have become. I have followed many of them from their days on Greenway Drive… through their school days and into their careers. I have heard it said that it takes a community to raise a child. I believe that there is much truth in that statement. I also know that those of us who were adults back then must have done a good job, because our Greenway Drive kids have made positive impacts everywhere they went. A lot of talent and a lot of good came from our neighborhood.

I am going to mention many of those kids who had an impact on my life. Ingram Truluck will always be remembered as the snake charmer. It is because of Ingram giving my son Stan a snake that I was able to get over my fear of snakes. I still respect them but no longer fear them. I will always remember Ingram's brother Johnny as a great athlete. Johnny was also in my Boy Scout troop, Troop 501. Andy and Danny Sansbury were also in my Scout troop. Andy was the first from Troop 501 to become an Eagle Scout. Danny is a preacher in Hartsville.

Stan with a snake.

Evalyn Kilgo had a big, solid-black racking horse named Ebony. She shared her barn with Stan and Rick when they got a horse for Christmas. Robin Mills and her family introduced me and my family to tent camping, something that we have done for many years since. Robin was so smart. Last I heard she was a big wheel in the state government. The Dewitt brothers were all good boys and grew into good men—Winkie, Tom, and Jim. They were good neighbors, very respectful and helpful. Betsy was just a baby when we moved to Darlington. She turned out to be a great kindergarten teacher for me at Pate School. She married David Forest, and they have spent a major portion of their lives traveling around this great country of ours. I'm sure she has been spreading a little Greenway Drive-ism along the way. Pete and Jeff Sansbury lived across the street and spent a lot of time playing at our house. Pete became a famous psychologist they say. Jeff is still around...living out on the Timmonsville highway. I have lost contact with the Lynch girls, Sue and Peggy. I heard

46

that Brent Sansbury was a successful car dealer in Lexington, South Carolina. He probably still has a scar on his face where my son Ricky bit him when they were playing together as toddlers.

Wayne Howle is a financial advisor. He must be pretty good because he had his picture on a whole billboard. His brother Ken was one of the most successful basketball coaches in the history of the school in Darlington. Ken used to come over and eat breakfast with Ricky. He loved Kool-Aid and Merle's breakfast specialty, milk gravy and crackers. The Bonnoitt girls, Linda and Sandra, were the best babysitters on Greenway Drive. Punk and Bimmy were in my Scout troop. Punk is a very successful plumber in town, and Bimmy worked his way up in the railroad business. I consider them both close adult friends today. Billy and Sarah Cain lived in the first house on the left when you turn onto Greenway Drive. Billy is a renown optometrist in South Carolina. Sarah was in one of my first classes at Brunson-Dargan Junior High. Everyone remembers the Cain vineyard. Robbie and Jimbo Brown lived beside us growing up. Robbie worked for the school district, and I think Jimbo was involved in real estate and housing somewhere on the coast.

Our other neighbors were the Bryants, and they became like family to us and still are to this day. Kenny always wanted to go places with my boys and me, so I started taking him. The first time was to the Sun 'n' Splash pool. He dove off the side, hit his head, and had to get stitched up. The second trip was to ride horses. The horse ran away with him, and he jumped off on a dirt road…back to the hospital. Even though he is an adult, I still won't take him anywhere with me.

I know that is not all of the children, but at eighty-nine years old, my memory isn't what it used to be. All I know is that I loved all the kids on Greenway Drive. Matter of fact, all the kids of Darlington and I have been so blessed to have been part of this community, this town, and Greenway Drive. I have been all over this world and have lived in California; Tennessee; Great Falls, South Carolina; Columbia, South Carolina; and Newberry, South Carolina; and I truly believe that Greenway Drive, Darlington, South Carolina, in the 1950s and 1960s was as good as it gets and a great place to raise a family.

Fran Wall Weaver

Evans Circle (aka Street)

Mother, Cyndie, and I returned to the Greenway Drive neighborhood in 1957. This move came after the death of my thirty-two-year-old father. He had fought battles in World War II at Guadalcanal, Cape Gloucester, and Peleliu, and was wounded twice and earned two Purple Hearts. He also fought a full year in hopes of winning his battle with stomach cancer. His Marine Corps training taught him to stick to the bitter end; and on February 27, 1957, when his 196-pound frame had reduced to 98 pounds, his battle was over. He had fought the good fight. My wise, strong, brave Mother brought my sister Cyndie and me right back to the neighborhood we had adored in 1954–1955. This was eight-year-old Cyndie's fourteenth move and my ninth as a four-year-old. We had rejoined the wondrous neighborhood which is like no other. This was a true "homecoming." Mother bought a sweet, perfect little house on Evans Circle with a purchase price of $9,000 and an interest rate of 4 percent.

This was the first and only home she owned. It was an exciting day when the moving truck arrived on Evans. Our household goods had been in storage for six months, and I was anxious to receive my red bike. I went to my knees when it came off the truck. It had shrunk, and there was no way I was going to be able to keep up with the other kids, especially in the curve of Evans Circle where the Scott's little brick retainer wall collected an abundance of sand on the road. Somehow, I managed, and we received one of our best gifts ever! Once again, we were among the attentive, devoted neighbors and friends who had greeted us with love and great care during our previous stay on Greenway Drive. Talented mentors were abundant in our neighborhood. This conglomeration of mentors consisted of school and Sunday school teachers, coaches, principals, social workers, bankers, jewelers, restaurant owners and managers, Welcome Wagon hostess, postal employees, highway department foreman, secretaries, scout leaders, car dealers, salesmen, attorneys, pharmacists, over-the-road truck drivers, a full-time reservist, and a tax collector. All parents watched over all children, and believe me, all children answered to all parents. You best not mess up there. Added to the parental blessings were the abundant environmental gifts in our area. We frolicked in a wonderland; with creeks running through the backyard and side yard, four ponds, woods, and a barn. A seventy-acre nature preserve named Williamson Park offered three creeks, over three hundred nature plants, many animal species, and a hill perfect for skateboarding (thank you, Margaret and Bright Williamson, for this exceptional gift).

In addition, we could walk to St. John's Elementary and High School, Brunson-Dargan Junior High, Spring Elementary, the little store (Parnell's/Turner's) at the foot of the hill on Main, the Sun 'n' Splash Pool, downtown, and the Blue Street recreational ball field. And, yes, we did have many chores—one was taking Mother's butterbeans to the field to shell while watching the game! With sixty-five kids, there was never a shortage of friends to play with. Everyone outside of our neighborhood wanted to be invited to play in our backyards. We developed our own sound system to alert others we were outside and ready for fun. "E-O-Weet" was the noise you created in the very back of your throat to send out the distinct yell. It could be heard throughout the neighborhood. Our days were filled with childhood games—cowboys and Indians, red rover, hide-and-seek, one two three red light, and ain't no boogers out tonight. And, yes, Jimbo Brown provided us entertainment on his screened-in porch casino. He taught us to gamble, gave prizes to winners, and sold frozen popsicles from his chest freezer. We also slid off the barn roof at the Kilgos'. (By the way, Evalyn and I rode her king-size horse, Ebony, bareback to Blue Street; her father, Bob, taught me Sunday School; her mother, Sis, could flat out dance the Charleston; and brother, Bobby, sure could run track.) We had BB guns, slingshots, hideouts, tunnels, and tree houses. We played basketball, full-fledged tackle, and touch football; roller-skated; and held competition bike races. Goodness! We even harvested rabbit tobacco and then rolled and sold handmade cigarettes. Yes, the fire truck did visit more than once. We also chewed pine sap. We stuck our tongues out, said, "I dare you," "Try it," and "Make me!" There was a desire to win at any cost. Some days, it was the girls against the boys, and sometimes, we chose sides.

Some of us stayed on restriction. I must admit at times we were a bit naughty. Tootsie Howle would call and then call again for Wayne and Ken to come home for supper. Seems they never answered, so we took on answering for them by yelling, "COMING!" I am not sure how much trouble we caused them, but I sure do want to take this opportunity to apologize now! Often, we lived off the land: ate plums, grapes, pecans, persimmons, and sour weeds. We were too busy playing outside to go inside to eat. We were yard monkeys. However, more often than not, we were thoughtful, said, "Pretty please," took up for one another, saved one another, were peacemakers, gave hugs, shared, were cheerful, were loyal, celebrated together, and cheered each other on with a sincere spirit of cooperation.

Stan Drawdy

Southern Delicacies

Most of us who lived on Greenway Drive would probably say we were middle-class folks. We didn't have everything we wanted, but we had the things we needed. None of us ever did without food, except by choice. In those days, at 112 Greenway Drive, my dad was the house breakfast cook. Mom worked also; and Dad did our breakfasts so that Mom could have time to get ready, get her makeup on, and be on time for work. If I had to select a word to describe Dad's cooking, it would be "creative." Many of our favorite breakfasts may sound a bit strange and unique to the average person, but to me and Rick, these dishes bring back many great memories. Even today, we still consider them delicacies and often have cooked them for children and grandchildren. Some of the children on Greenway Drive may have been lucky enough to have eaten breakfast at the Drawdy house and may have shared one of the family favorites with us.

Here are some of our favorites:

1. Milk Gravy and Crackers: This dish consists of crumbled saltine crackers, covered with a big helping of homemade sawmill gravy. The gravy is made from sausage or bacon grease and white flour and milk…or water if no milk is available. This is the very same flour and water that we made homemade glue with for building kites, and completing homework assignments that required glue.

2. Cornbread Cush: This lovely dish is made from leftover cornbread, warmed up in a cast-iron skillet with but-

51

ter (definitely not real butter but rather the manmade kind). Then add eggs, and scramble the entire concoction together until the eggs are done. Add more butter to individual taste.

3. Rocky Mountain Toast: This is a simple version of French toast, was sold to us as a favorite of mountain hikers and campers. It consisted of one piece of light bread with a hole about the size of a half dollar pinched out of the middle. Place the "holey" bread in a cast-iron skillet; crack one egg into the center of the hole; and fry it in butter until the egg is done—fried, over easy, or sunny side up. Served with honey, jam, or plain.

4. Fried Grits (Harve's favorite): Leftover grits from "breakfast-for-supper night." Chilled overnight in the fridge. Then cut into squares, and then fried in butter (you know) until golden brown.

5. Hot Chocolate and Toast: Piping hot, hot chocolate and buttered toast. Dip the buttered toast into the hot chocolate before eating. Delicioso!

6. Harve's Hash: Served on toast, this brown meat hash was one of our favorites until one day Dad told us what they called it when he was in the armed forces: "___ on a shingle." (You can fill in the blank).

7. Hunter's Stew: This delicacy could be, and often was, served for any meal; and it was a family favorite. Not because it was good but because it was what we were told that "true hunters" ate. This dish was basically all the vegetables that were left over from previous meals, all mixed together, with a can of Campbell's soup (doesn't matter which kind). Hunter's Stew never tasted the same as the last Hunter's Stew that we had. But if hunters can eat it, so can we.

We had other, more traditional breakfasts from time to time; but they deserve no mention, since they offer no originality.

Many times during the year, we were treated to some of Dad's wild game dishes. On Saturday evenings and during holidays, he and

Kenneth were always cooking up fish or squirrel stews, whatever they had caught or killed that day. Sometimes, they would cook venison, but that was very rare, because neither of them was very good at deer hunting. Actually, you had a better chance of spotting Sasquatch than seeing either of them kill a deer. But possums and raccoons were pretty common, on the weekend, at Harvey's shop.

There was one more Southern delicacy worth mentioning—one that all of us on Greenway Drive enjoyed from time to time. This was probably the best of all, and was prepared and then brought to the neighborhood by the one we commonly referred to as "the Man on the Bicycle." On occasions, he would ride his bike through the neighborhood, literally pedaling his products in small brown bags for twenty-five cents per bag. The wire basket attached to the handlebars of his bike would be full of small brown bags, filled with…boiled peanuts! What a treat! What a Southern delicacy!

Keith Carter

Zig Ziglar Cooked Our Dinner

The name Zig Ziglar is known to a lot of Americans, and many would say his name is a household name. He was a highly successful salesperson who became a motivational speaker and entertainer in his second career, which is how he became so well-known all across the country. As a natural salesman with the gift of gab, he capitalized on his personality and success by teaching other people to do the same, whether in sales or in any walk of life. Even though he has passed away, I still see his quotes that people post on Facebook, which are always simple, sensible, and meaningful; and there is a Facebook page in the name of "Zig Ziglar" since his motivation company still exists. It's amazing how one person can have the insight and ability to put their knowledge into understandable words and market them, which he did during his illustrious life. He died at the age of eighty-six, highly successful in everything he attempted to do.

My mother reminded us years later, after he became famous, that she remembered the day he knocked on our door on Greenway Drive, in early 1956. Since our house was near Spring Street, it was likely the first one he encountered on our street where someone was at home. He was selling Wear-Ever aluminum cookware, and his sales pitch was simple: he showed my mother some of his pots and pans, then told her that he would come back and cook dinner on our stove if she would invite several neighboring housewives over to join us. She told me later that he was so personable and likable that she did not hesitate in picking up the phone and inviting friends on our street. The families on our street were about the same ages, the husbands having been in World War II, then marrying, buying houses just as millions did all over the country, and having children. Zig was also in this age group, being the same age as my dad and having been in the Navy, so he had credibility in that area too.

I did some research and found that Zig attended college at the University of South Carolina after the war and then took a job with Wear-Ever and moved to Lancaster, South Carolina, and then a year or two later to Florence, South Carolina, which is where he lived when he called on us. Zig provided the food for the meal he cooked, choosing items which would demonstrate the versatility of the pots, which included tricks like stacking two pots to make a sort of double boiler. Although the meal was almost ready when our neighbors showed up, he took some time to show what he had prepared and how he had done it, always stressing the simplicity and versatility of the cookware he was there to sell. He even demonstrated how easy it was to clean the fabulous cookware, by washing them all himself, talking and joking the whole time! I have vague memories about the whole thing, including the novelty of a man in our kitchen, cooking with brand-new pots and pans, talking a lot, all while being likable and entertaining the ladies. My mother bought a set (of course) when his presentation was over. I can't tell you how many other mothers also bought—I can only guess—maybe all of them. Peer pressure, you know, creates a powerful sales tool, something Zig had figured out. He became a top salesman for the Wear-Ever Company.

I remember the pots very well; they were cast aluminum and rather thick walled, with Bakelite handles. The lids were thinner than the pots and had round Bakelite knobs. Another thing I remember is that my mother warped her favorite small pot a few years later by throwing it at a dog who was rummaging through our trash can just outside the kitchen door (he was a repeat offender). The shape of the pot changed that day from round to somewhat egg shaped (from hitting the ground, not the dog), and she asked Daddy to beat it back into shape. He tried, but the lid would no longer fit. My parents used that set of pots and pans for many decades, and they were like a part of the family. She often mentioned Zig since he was just that way—unforgettable. She was delighted when he became famous, since she remembered him "way back when" on Greenway Drive, before he hit the big time.

Zig's career morphed into a second phase when he began selling his sales secrets to the world. His new company began with his motivational speechmaking and seminars, and in 1975, he wrote his best-selling book, *See You at the Top*. He went on to write a total of thirty books and sold millions of audio and video cassette tapes of his techniques, secrets, and quotes. Those later turned into CDs and DVDs, which still sell, along with his books. The man was a motivational machine and created an empire and quite a legacy. He always stressed that the secret of good salesmanship was really no secret at all—his techniques were open and available to anyone who took the time to buy his methods and put them to work. His naturally cheerful, honest, homey, and morally guided manner made him a uniquely qualified public speaker, regardless of the audience. He told his story on countless TV shows which showcased his entertaining style for audience appeal. And he never lost his folksy Southern humor, charm, and manners. For a taste, go to YouTube and enter his name, and then watch and listen to some of his speeches. Now every time I see a quote from Zig Ziglar, I smile and think to myself: he was great but never any greater than the evening he cooked dinner in our house on Greenway Drive!

Bobby Kilgo

The Fifth Kilgo

We arrived on Greenway Drive in October 1958. My father had inherited around five acres from his father. Prior to the completion of the new house, there were only a horse barn, pond, and smokehouse on the property. There were five of us. Bob and Sis were my parents. Evalyn was my sister. I was nine and in the fourth grade. Evalyn was seven and in the second grade. The house was constructed on the back side of the property facing the pond.

The fifth person was Lizzie Perkins Johnson. She lived north of the city with her husband, Nathaniel, and their three children. This story is about Lizzie and my experiences in Darlington. They began before we arrived on Greenway Drive. Some of you who read this will know the stories, but I hope to enlighten you about this wonderful woman.

When my parents brought me home from the adoption agency, I was three months old. My parents were each thirty-three years of age. They had been married for seven years. Their hopes of a natural child had waned. Sis was not prepared for this new responsibility. She needed help. As January 1950 ended, she was head over heels in diapers, crying baby, and caring for Bob and our dog, Judge.

On a cold February morning, there was a knock at the front door. Mother answered it, and a tall heavyset black woman was standing on the other side of the screen door. The woman introduced herself and said, "Mrs. Kilgo, I understand you need some help." That began an over-thirty-year relationship. Lizzie was in charge of the house, and especially me!

Lizzie was at the house six days a week. The highlight was the Saturday midday meal. Daddy would work in the morning, and when he arrived home, we ate in the breakfast room nook in the kitchen. The vegetables, starches, and desserts would vary; but there was always fried chicken and biscuits. Four of us would be at the table and Lizzie across the counter on a stepstool. All five of us ate and conversed about the week that had passed and what the next week held for us.

Lizzie only corrected me on a few occasions. She was my guardian. If she did have to admonish me, I usually responded with eye movement. That was my signal of disgust, but hers was always, "Don't you cut your eyes at me, Bob!" I can hear her say that to this day.

Lizzie lived on a farm. Many times, Evalyn and I would go to her house to visit. Nathaniel's farm equipment was old. It had been through several owners before he could afford it. I loved sitting on his tractor and pretending I was plowing a row of tobacco or cotton. That was as close as I ever came to doing agricultural work.

As a farmer's wife, she had learned many skills. One was the proper way to cure country ham. Daddy would buy several hams, and Lizzie was in charge afterward. She prepared them for curing, hung them in the smokehouse, and watched as they changed from a plain ham to one a Southerner would enjoy. She would make red-eye gravy to accompany it. Later, Evalyn's husband continued the recipe he learned from her.

My father, an avid outdoorsman, introduced me to fishing on our pond. I did not like it. Paddling the boat was fun, but throwing a line to catch bream was boring. He tried me with golf, but I was stubborn. Being left-handed, I did not do well with right-handed clubs. Also, I just did not like to expend energy on anything but reading and riding my bicycle. One time, to get me outside, he instructed me to pick up the pine cones in the yard. I was so frustrated I just sat on the back porch. Lizzie came to my rescue. She coaxed me out to the yard, and we picked them up as a team. We were always a team.

Our paved circle became a bicycle racetrack for the neighborhood. I am sure others have written about those days when Fireball Roberts Truluck or Joe Weatherly Sansbury took to the track for the

Southern 500. Lizzie was always there to watch and make sure we had some iced tea or lemonade to drink.

Evalyn fussed many times that I was Lizzie's favorite. Of course, I denied it. But Evalyn was probably right. I think Lizzie just liked boys and men better than girls and women. One time, my mother and Lizzie got into an argument, and Lizzie quit. It took Mr. Bob to get her back.

One memory I have is of November 22, 1963. I was playing hooky from school. Lizzie was ironing clothes, and I was on the couch. We had the television on, and we heard from Walter Cronkite that President John F. Kennedy had been killed in Dallas. I remember Lizzie weeping quietly as we learned of what had happened. There was complete stillness.

Lizzie and Nathaniel sharecropped for Ed Howle. Later, they purchased their farm from him. The home and the fifty-five acres of farmland still remain in the family. Nathaniel died in 1971. He provided for his family in a will my father prepared. Rubye received the homeplace with a proviso Lizzie could stay there until her death. That happened in November 1983. She had been a loyal member of New Hopewell Missionary Baptist Church in Antioch. Her funeral was there, and she is buried in the church cemetery. A sacred place for a soulful lady.

Danny Sansbury

When Mama Killed the Copperhead

We were playing in our front yard, which was located about halfway from Spring Street to the Kilgo (Spooky) Barn, which more or less marked the end of our memorable street. Our yard was also the most open yard in the neighborhood—most other yards had some or a lot of trees in them. That allowed our yard to be the open venue for countless games of kickball, crack the whip, football, baseball (plastic ball and bat), and much more.

One afternoon, while a group of us were playing, Ingram Truluck raced into the yard on his bicycle. He called out to everyone, "There's a copperhead snake in our yard!" Of course, on reflection, such a declaration had to come from Ingram. After all, he had a snake collection in wooden boxes about four feet off the ground in his backyard. It was Ingram who had ordered a boa constrictor delivered to his house one spring. That boa was shown around the neighborhood. The boa escaped somehow, and little children were warned that it might come up out of the woods and constrict one of us. Fortunately for us, the boa was never seen again.

That afternoon, all the children in the Sansbury front yard ran down the street, past the Welch house, to see the copperhead by a large pine tree near the street of the Trulucks' yard. As we circled around to see this poisonous serpent, out of the crowd came my mother, Mary Anne. She had heard Ingram's declaration in the front yard. She had raced through our garage and grabbed the shovel. Then she caught up with us as we stared at the copperhead. This was the only time that a poisonous snake was sighted in someone's front yard. As we watched in awe, down came the shovel from this tall woman onto the unsuspecting snake. Down it came again and again as my mother, on behalf of all protective mothers on Greenway Drive, whacked the snake into bloody pieces. She was the Avenging Angel on this demon snake that dared to enter our safe neighborhood and threaten the many children living and playing there. Its violent end served as a brutal warning to any other poisonous snakes who might want to enter our play areas.

Addendum 1: my mother devised a snake-catching tool with an adjustable string on the end of a former broomstick. She used that tool, and taught us to use it, to catch a number of garter or hognose snakes found in our woods between our house and the creek. She also made a wooden box to keep the captured snakes for several days. She wanted us to learn not to be afraid of snakes and to be able to identify them. What a contrast to what happened when a copperhead was identified in the Trulucks' front yard!

Addendum 2: I took one of those captured snakes to "Show and Tell" at Spring Elementary School. I was in third grade in Mrs. Fletcher's class. I brought a mud snake, a very tame reptile. Not everyone in third grade had a mother like mine. So not everyone was happy to see a snake at "Show and Tell" that day.

Stan Drawdy

The Spooky Old Barn

O ne of my favorite places on Greenway Drive was the Kilgos' barn. Many of us referred to that old barn as the Spooky Barn. It really wasn't very spooky, but it was a place where we often tried to prank other kids by telling them it was haunted, then have someone hide in it and try and scare those that we brought over to see it. Once we told some kids that Johnny had fallen off the roof of the barn and he was hurt bad and we needed help. When we got there, Johnny was lying in a pool of blood (water and ketchup). It looked kinda real from a distance, but once we got closer, you could tell it wasn't real. Plus it was hard to keep from laughing.

Another thing about that barn was that it was where a local Boy Scout troop held their weekly meetings. That part of the barn stayed locked up all the time, and it was "almost" impossible to get into. You could see through the cracks in the boards of the barn walls into their meeting room. It looked pretty interesting with flags, posters, etc. on the interior walls. Sometimes, we would be standing across the drive in Pete and Jeff's yard while they were meeting and could clearly see into the room. I don't know if any of the kids in our neighborhood were actually in that Boy Scout troop. I think most of the kids on Greenway Drive were in my dad's troop, Troop 501, and they met at First Baptist Church. Two Cub Scout troops were formed on Greenway Drive; one was Mary Anne Sansbury's troop, and the other was Jackie Sansbury's. The Cub Scouts met at the leaders' houses.

The barn was also used as a barn for horses. Evalyn Kilgo had a racking horse named Ebony. Ebony stayed in one of the stalls on the backside of the barn. Later when Rick and I got our horse, Brandy, the Kilgos allowed us to keep her in one of the stalls on the front side of the barn. Both sides of the barn had small tack rooms for saddles and bridles, hay, and feed. Brandy turned out to be a mean horse, and Dad sold her and got a male horse that was good and gentle. His name was Dan. Dan stayed in the old barn until we moved out in the country. I cannot remember any other horses that were boarded in that old barn, but I heard that there were several there at one time many years before.

The best thing about the old barn was the roof. The tin roof was the perfect roof for kids to play on. A tin roof makes a perfect sliding board, especially when you take an empty burlap feed sack, sit on it, and lift your feet. You could also grab up a bundle of straw or hay and sit on it. Sliding on hay might have even created a faster slide than the empty sacks. But the problem wasn't sliding; it was landing. It must have been about an eight-foot drop from the edge of the roof to the ground, and the ground around the barn was pretty hard. It did not take us long to figure out we needed to land in a pile of hay or straw. Sometimes, we raked up pine straw to land in, and sometimes, we landed in the piles of hay and manure from where they cleaned out the horse stalls. Sliding the barn roof was a great thrill, but like anything good, there were pitfalls, and we suffered them all. Sprains and broken bones were rare, but they did occur. To me, the scariest and most difficult thing to avoid was getting cut by a sharp edge of the tin or by a nail sticking up that was not nailed down tight. Rusty nails, rusty tin, and landing on manure piles, plus cuts on your feet and legs, equaled a trip to Dr. Wilson and a tetanus shot. At least that's the way it usually worked out in my family.

Spooky Barn.

I remember one time I got a cut on my leg under my pants, and I didn't tell anyone, especially Mom. I tried to doctor it myself with stuff in the medicine cabinet. Mom must have figured it out that I was injured, because she asked me several times that night if I was cut. I kept telling her no, because I didn't want to get a shot. She warned me that if I was cut, that I could get "lockjaw." She said that it would cause your jaws to lock and you would never be able to open your mouth again to eat or to talk and that once they lock up, even the doctors couldn't fix it. That night, I worried so much about lockjaw that I kept testing my jaws by wiggling them back and forth, and opening them as wide as I could. I kept testing them about every twenty minutes all that evening until I fell asleep. When I woke up the next morning, my jaws were as sore as they could be. My only thought was that I was getting lockjaw. I had no choice except to fess up to Mom. I showed her my Spooky Barn injury, and she showed me the way to Dr. Wilson's office, and he showed me what a tetanus shot felt like. Soon I stopped testing my jaws, and the soreness went away. I was cured!

That old Spooky Barn will always be remembered by those of us on Greenway Drive. Some will remember it as a meeting place. Some remember it as a fun place. Some remember it as a scary place, and some remember it as a dangerous place. No matter how one remembers it, it was a part of our past, and I find it hard to think of Greenway Drive without thinking of that old barn.

Tree House Builders

One of my favorite shows to watch is *Pete Nelson and the Tree House Builders*. In the show, they travel around the country building luxury tree houses for people. The show starts out with Pete meeting the customers, and then he goes onto the property. They locate a perfect place to build, Pete designs the new structure, and then his crew comes in and builds it. Before it is unveiled to the new owners, it is furnished and decorated. The new owners are then brought out with eyes closed for the reveal. They count to 3, they open their eyes, and the finished product is seen. Right before their eyes sits a fantasy tree house—a dream house built in the trees. It is truly amazing how the tree houses turn out.

Well, in the early to mid-1960s, Greenway Drive had its own tree house builders; and they built a three-story wonder, deep in Kilgos' woods. You know you could cut through the Kilgos' woods, then cross a very small field that was grown up in weeds and then a row of old houses where "Porkchop" and some of our other black friends lived, cross over Blue Street, and you would be standing on the Pony League baseball field behind Spring School. Well, the tree house was built right at the end of the woods, just before it turned into the small grown-up field. The tree house was pretty, and it was built by some of the older boys. It was kind of a work in progress because kids didn't have money to buy materials back then, so they mostly used their dad's tools and scrap lumber, plus screws and nails that might be lying around in someone's shop. You might say that the Greenway Drive tree house started with just one floor. It looked like a plywood box stuck between three or four trees. The front had a big opening that stretched across, so you could see the little overgrown field toward

Blue Street. The other three sides were closed in. There was an opening in the flooring, just big enough for big kids to climb through, and the roof had a similar opening that led to the second story. On top of the second story was the third, and final, story. The two additional stories were additions to the original first floor, and the timing of the additions coincided with new home constructions or additions on or near Greenway Drive. You see, new construction in the neighborhood meant scrap wood and materials, which are what were mostly used to build the tree house and additions to it. Most construction work took place while we were in school, and was not going on Saturdays, which was exactly when kids could find the scrap materials needed to build. Most of the materials came from the scrap piles, but occasionally, one might have to borrow from a different pile.

The first time I saw the tree house, I was with Johnny. I think he might have been in the original building. We climbed from the ground all the way to the top of the third story. That's when I met Porkchop, a kid who lived on Blue Street. Johnny already knew him, but that was the first time I had ever seen him. Later on, when we walked over to the Pony League field to play ball (when the field was vacant), Porkchop and some of the other kids on Blue Street would come over and play with us. I also remember one time near Christmas, my mom was reading the paper, and she told me about a kid on Blue Street who had been accidentally shot while playing with a gun in his house. She read his name, but I didn't recognize it. Mom told me I was to never play with any real guns, ever; they were for hunting only; and only when I was with Dad. I wondered if the kid who died was Porkchop, because I never saw him again after that. Years later, I learned it was Porkchop.

I do not remember much more about the old tree house, but every time I see the show *Treehouse Builders*, I think about that three-story tree house back in Kilgos' woods. I think about me and Johnny and Porkchop climbing all through that kid-built structure. I think about my first black friend. And I wonder…are there tree houses in heaven? If so, I bet there are amazing tree houses like the ones built by Pete Nelson. I also bet Johnny and Porkchop have already climbed through them and checked them out! Or maybe not…maybe they are waiting on me to join them.

Cynthia Wall Geries

Greenway Drive Part 1

If the Kilgos' barn could talk, it would share lots of secrets. Those green pine cone fights caused Evalyn and me to often retreat to our secret fort in the woods behind their house heading toward Blue Street. The Kilgos' front yard served to host neighborhood kickball games many Sunday afternoons. I will never forget Howard or Lizzie. As Howard was regularly gathering pine straw, we would hide behind the big pine trees and eavesdrop. Howard constantly talked to himself as he worked. Lizzie provided us with flour and spices as we concocted blobs of biscuits to cook in Evalyn's Easy Bake Oven. Don't tell anyone, but Evalyn and I regularly took the boat out without permission. I think that Barbara Truluck stowed away with us on occasion. Where should I begin with stories and shared memories of the Truluck family? Ingram was the man, our leader, the Southern 500 organizer, and nature boy with all of his snakes. I must not forget how he and Leonard Ballard orchestrated annual car races, bicycle races, the parades, and all other related festivities.

Sitting on our screened porch making an endless number of potholders to sell was a hot venture during the summer. The money earned would serve to finance our next neighborhood project. Among the projects, I remember charging ten cents per doll carriage ride down the hill in our backyard and across the creek. Speaking of the creek, I wonder how many turtles, salamanders, and frogs we caught. As a result of exploring woods, the creek, and the park, I was constantly covered in poison oak/ivy. I also remember gathering straw and digging tunnels on the vacant lot across the street from our

house. This lot was eventually purchased by Mae and Cleve Scott.
They built a brick ranch-style house. We were so excited the night
Helen Scott got married at their home. I also recall that Sandra Scott
and Robbie Brown played high school tennis. Judy Scott was born
when Clyde, Helen, and Sandra were older. I can still see Judy standing in the playpen in their den. I will never forget the throw that Mae
crocheted and gifted to me when I was grown. Her divinity candy
was the best ever and always a welcomed Christmas gift to our family.
Mae and mother enjoyed a lifelong friendship after all children were
grown and gone.

Back row: Diane Pate, Sarah Cain, Cyndie Wall, and Sandra Bonnoitt.
Middle row: Fran Wall, Linda Bonnoitt, Andy
Sansbury, and Barbara Truluck.
Front row: Mikey Bonnoitt (visiting cousin).

Before the Powers built a home between the Cains and the Bonnoitts, we played on the lot under a huge walnut tree. Bunny was always game for fun. I remember riding up to BC Moore's with her and the girls. She purchased a pair of shoes that she could use to join us for roller-skating in the street. Bunny often let the girls open a window so we could hear the radio/record player as we danced and tumbled on their front lawn.

I spent many days at Lottie and Kenneth Bryant's house. Lottie was a fabulous cook and especially good at frying the fish Kenneth caught. I have fond memories of strolling Sandra and Patricia up and down Greenway Drive. I must admit that Patricia got beyond her fair share of strolling ventures because she had colic and was subject to frequent crying spells! Kenny was yet to be born. I remember occasional rides to school in Sly and Tootsie Dewitt's car in a rumble seat. Winkie and Tom were our good friends. I think that carpool was before Betsy was born. I enjoyed trying to catch fish in their pond too. Speaking of their pond, I have memories of walking home from Brunson-Dargan Junior High down Doneraile Street, where some of the scenes from the movie *Thunder in Carolina* were filmed. We crossed over N. Main Street and cut through the Dewitts' uncle's yard that backed up to their pond. As I recall, some of our Southern 500 bike races were held near their driveway. Other races took place along the outside fence line of Brent Sansbury's yard and behind Pete and Jeff Sansbury's yard. Those races were a creative group effort consisting of decorating bikes, creating floats, and awarding trophies. Parade floats were created from strollers, carriages, tricycles, wagons, and various other concoctions with wheels. Ingram Truluck and Leonard Ballard usually served as the announcers with their radio voices. We were creative in all endeavors and took great pride in our accomplishments.

The end of Greenway Drive was also the location of Robin Mill's home. She was a great playmate. I think we wore out her record player to the tune of "Running Bear."

Pinehaven Avenue was home to many friends. Lee and Samara Beckham once lived at the end of the street. Barbara Morris, who was Dr. Wilson's nurse, lived with her family directly behind us. She was quick to the rescue when Fran once ate a box of Ex-Lax, thinking it was chocolate candy. Barbara whipped up some soapy dishwater and made Fran drink it. It didn't take long before the Ex-Lax was expelled. I will never forget that the Jack Morris family used a sweet potato in the place of the missing gas cap on their car. They were a fun family who moved to Charleston after a brief stay in the neighborhood. Their daughter, Glinda Dell, was a good friend.

Christmas memories never cease to amaze me. When Daddy was on a tour of Japan in the Marine Corps, I was in the first grade and part of the second grade. We were new to Greenway Drive and rented a house next door to Nancy, Jimmy, Robbie, and Jimbo Brown. The Bonnoitts and Sansburys lived across the street from us. I think we had the best Christmas ever except for the fact that Daddy was deployed. Jimmy Brown and Johnny Bonnoitt helped assemble our doll bed, doll high chair, toy piano, and other treasures late on Christmas Eve. Uncle Claud and Aunt Betty lived on Pinehaven. We moved to Darlington to have family nearby while Daddy was on assignment. Uncle Claud was always our "second dad" and made beautiful glass doll cases for the Japanese dolls that Daddy mailed to Fran and me. He sent Mom a Japanese music box that held cigarettes that moved up and down as the music played. We loved the Japanese pajamas he mailed, although they were a bit too big.

Another family on Pinehaven next door to Aunt Betty and Uncle Claud Smith were the Smyres. We loved playing with Dane and Cynthia, and much later Jan came along. When they built their new house on Medford, I remember babysitting there.

Bill and Beulah Dubose, who lived on Spring Street, were especially good to us. They made the best bread and butter pickles ever. We played with Grady and Danny Dubose regularly. I remember riding to the country with them on Saturdays to "take the trash." Their grandparents had a pump in their kitchen, and I had my first drink from a dipper at their country home. The Dubose family was very loyal to our family especially, in the absence and early death of Daddy. They visited us at Camp Lejeune in Jacksonville, North Carolina, after Daddy came home from Japan. Dad was diagnosed with stomach cancer and eventually died from this brutal disease at age thirty-two. Upon his death in 1957, we returned to Darlington where my remarkable mother purchased our house on Evans Circle from the Jeffords family. We were welcomed back to the neighborhood and made more memories to last a lifetime. So many families provided friendships and memories that, indeed, lasted a lifetime.

Keith Carter

Cutto Mickey

While growing up, we were taught to never curse, swear, or use the Lord's name in vain. This was an absolute dictum, and I think my brother and I did pretty good abiding by this rule. My sister, Shelley, was three and a half years younger than me; and I don't think she was even told about this rule. Telling her not to cuss would have been like telling a jellyfish not to jaywalk.

I remember the morning on Greenway Drive like it was yesterday. It was the last day of school before the Christmas holidays; and we were just finishing breakfast when we heard firecrackers going off, one after another, coming up the street toward our house. My mother looked through the venetian blinds and saw a neighbor kid, Leonard "Leo" Ballard, who was lighting firecrackers with a punk stick, holding them until the fuse had burned halfway down and then throwing them so they would explode in midair. If you lit them and threw them quickly, they would hit the ground before going off because they didn't weigh enough to go very far, and that wasn't satisfying at all. Besides, the midair bang created firecracker confetti, which was a bonus. So the daring "light and hold for a second" routine was common among the big boys.

I went outside to watch this exciting fun. I would have been in about the second grade, seven years old, and Leo was four years older. At eleven, he was definitely a "big boy" to me. He lived around the corner and up Spring Street, which was isolated compared to Greenway Drive with its postwar litters of baby boom kids, but we certainly knew him. He had come to our street to cause a sensation on this last morning before the two-week Christmas holidays that we all anticipated so highly.

Leo was getting bolder with the delay between the lighting and the throwing of the firecrackers, and having an admiring audience of short little people only fueled his courage. He would hold the firecrackers until the fuse had burned even more than halfway down before throwing them, and they were exploding very soon after he threw them. Finally, he got too bold, and a firecracker went off before he could throw it. What I really remember is what he yelled, "GOT-toe MIGHT-EEE!" as he grabbed his fingers with his other hand and then cried, "Ow! Ow! Ow!" as he hopped around; and I realized he was actually crying. I was astounded to see a big eleven-year boy crying, as I had thought someone that old was well beyond such a thing. He was in a lot of pain and just couldn't help it.

My mother heard the commotion from inside the house and correctly guessed what had happened since it fulfilled the expectation that all mothers have over firecrackers or anything else that's dangerous and fun. She grabbed a bottle of Watkins Liniment (which my father sold) and ran out to the street where Leo was still dancing around, squeezing his burned fingers and failing in his attempt not to cry in front of his fans; and she poured it over his hand. It must have helped immediately because he calmed down and seemed relieved, since he was trying hard to compose himself in front of my mother and his young admirers who were gathered around, wide-eyed and learning. I noticed his hurt fingers were black. His glory was sadly over, and he soon hightailed it back home, and we went back in the house. We still had to go to school.

I thought about what Leo had said in his flashing moment of pain: "Gotto Mighty." It was a new one to me. But I knew it had to be forbidden due to the way he had involuntarily blurted it out. Nobody says good words at a time like that. I cataloged it in the growing Mystery File. Later, the exclamation began cropping up from some of our other buddies. No one knew what was actually being said; so there were variations on how to say it—variations being "Gotto mighty," "Cotto modey," and "Cutto modey." It was said as someone would say, "Oh—my *good*ness!" or "Holy moly!" It became a sort of game among those who said it to see who could say it the funniest way. Exaggerating the pronunciation and delivering the words in staccato chops gave it the most meaning and brought the most admiration. It seems that the end of the line in the evolution was "*Cutto Mickey*," which could not be improved upon.

I don't think it ever entered the minds of any of us—certainly not me—that the expression had any connection with using the Lord's name in vain. I didn't realize for years that what was actually being said was, "God Almighty." We just instinctively knew it fell under the classification of "bad words" because it was never said around parents or teachers, only in isolation.

Some of our friends could openly and freely say such words as *darn* and *dern*, even around their parents. *Darn* was considered to be a mild, sissified bad word. *Dern* was a step up the ladder toward danger, and I later realized both were used as watered-down substitutes for the forbidden *damn*. And it was REALLY a major sin to put God's name in front of that one, and few in our circle of friends ever dared go that far. So *damn* was uttered only rarely and just on very special occasions, in the utmost privacy from grown-ups. Another innocent substitute word was "Shoot!"—not that we knew what it represented either, until some years later.

One epithet that entered our lexicon a little later in my childhood, believe it or not, was "Dag Hammarskjöld" (Hammershawl!) uttered in similar circumstances as "Cutto Mickey." Dag Hammarskjold was the name of the then leader of the United Nations, as we had learned in school from our Weekly Readers, and must have been discussed the day one of our buddies stepped in the creek with his shoe on or something. We liked the way it sounded, especially when accented on "Dag" and "Ham." The best part was that no one could accuse us of cussing; we were just discussing high-brow school stuff.

One day, I went to the door of a friend's home on the street (who shall remain nameless) to see if he could come out to play. He came out, shut the door, and said, "Dammit to hell."

I was stunned, and he saw it, so he boldly added, "Dammit to hell, anyway!" He looked very pleased with himself. I stammered, "Why are you saying that!" He scuffed the ground with his foot and said, "I don't know—just for the hell of it, I guess." Well! This was some serious cussing, and I half expected God to send a lightning bolt and strike him dead on the spot. I mean, blurting out bad words in a fit of pain or frustration was one thing, but saying it for no reason was pretty serious stuff in my book. But I soon learned that experimentation such as this was a part of growing up, and there were many more private rehearsals of cussing as life continued.

There came the evening when our family was sitting at the supper table and the blessing had been said. My brother Philip dipped out some hot macaroni and cheese and put a big bite into his mouth. "*Cut*-to *Mic*-key!" he let slip under his breath but audibly enough. With a scorched mouth, he grabbed his glass of tea for relief. My father, recognizing the expression for what it might mean, said, "You will not take the Lord's name in vain in this house!" as he glared at Philip with sternness in his voice, eyes, and jaw.

Philip looked back at him with a look that contained puzzlement as well as the pain from his burned mouth. Never a grammarian, he finally said, "But, Daddy! Cutto Mickey ain't no lord!"

Ring-Ring!

I am ancient enough to remember the days when we had a single black telephone in our house. It had no dial or push buttons, only a white circle on the front with the telephone number on it. There was a handheld receiver with a cord that was not coiled, thus was not stretchy. When you picked up the receiver and put it to your ear, a pleasant lady said, "Number, please." It was a real, live lady speaking. She worked in the telephone office in town, and her job was to connect you with the number you wanted to call. She was called the Operator. The only way to make a telephone call was to tell the Operator the number you wanted to call. It worked great!

When making a call and the Operator asked, "Number, please," it was preferable that you had the number you wanted to call; but if not, you could say, "I need the A&P Store," or "I need Dr. Wilson's office," and she would either know it by heart or would quickly look it up and connect you. We all had a small telephone book that listed all the phone numbers in town alphabetically, so it was easy to look up the number of who you wanted to call if you didn't know it. Telephone numbers could be as short as one digit but were also two, three, or four digits. I remember that Central Drugstore's phone number was 9—it was painted on the side of the building.

Phone numbers which were numeric only, that is, without a letter after them, were private lines. Most businesses had private lines, but many homes shared "party lines." For example, our telephone number in my early days on Greenway Drive was 1127-R. We shared a party line with the Smith family around the corner on Spring Street, who had the number 1127-W. When our phone rang with two shorts—*ring-ring*—we knew the call was for us, and we could answer the phone. When it rang with one long *ri-i-i-i-ng*, it was for the Smiths and we should not answer. The phones in each home rang every time either of our homes received a call. If we did pick up when the call was for the Smiths, we could hear their conversation, but it was impolite to do so. Nothing except good manners stopped either party from listening in when the other party was on the phone. Party lines between homes were basically like extensions or the multiple phones which became common in our homes later on.

If we wanted to make a call but heard a conversation going on after we picked up the receiver, it was polite to say, "Oops, sorry," or "I'll try later," and quietly hang up. If this was repeated every few minutes and they were still talking, they would either get the hint and finish their conversation, or they might say, "I'm sorry, but this is a very important call, so please give me a few more minutes," or "STOP picking up your PHONE while I'm TALKING!"—something to that effect. We never had any trouble with the Smiths, and I don't think they had any problem with the Carters, since most people were naturally courteous and respectful. But it could be a real aggravation to be on a call and hear someone of the other party continually pick up the receiver, interrupt, or not hang up but listen, especially if they were loud breathers.

There were two-party lines (as we had), and other multiples up to eight-party lines, especially out in the country. The monthly cost of the phone service went down with more parties on the line, with a private line being a luxury. Six- and eight-party lines were pretty cheap monthly, and rightly so.

In 1958, Darlington entered the modern age when Southern Bell gave us Dial Tone! This changed a lot of things: first, everyone got a new telephone which had a rotary dial on the front. We no longer placed calls with the help of an Operator but used the dial on the new phone to call the number we wanted. Second, we could get a telephone that was a color other than black, like green, red, yellow, or white; but they cost extra. Third, we could get a phone that hung on the wall instead of sitting on a table or countertop. Fourth, when the receiver was picked up and put to the ear, we heard something new—a steady hum that was called the Dial Tone. This meant the phone was connected and working properly. It was fun to pick up the phone just to listen to the soothing new dial tone (life was simple back then). Nothing changed about receiving a call, and the new dial service had no effect on party lines, which continued as before.

Perhaps the biggest change of all was that every home and business was given a new phone number, which took the most getting used to for grown-ups. Unlike before, when numbers could be anything from a single digit on up, now all numbers were a total of seven characters which included two letters and five numbers. The first three characters were common to everyone in Darlington and together were called the "prefix." Each town, or part of a larger town, was assigned a prefix word, which in Darlington was "Express," followed by "3." Following the prefix was the unique four-digit phone number, and local calls could be made using only those four digits. But when asked for our phone number, the correct answer was Express3-4498 or EX3-4498 or 393-4498—all were correct and were dialed the same. On the telephone dial, each digit had three letters with it, except the 1 and the 0; 0 was for calling an Operator, who still existed but presumably had much less to do. They provided assistance with problems, looking up numbers, and placing long-distance calls.

It became a fun exercise to find out the telephone prefix words of neighboring towns. Florence had Mohawk, and Hartsville had Fireside. Columbia had Alpine; and in Greenville, where I now live, the main one was Cedar. There were hundreds used all over the country.

Darlington's phone service was switched from the old system to the dial system on a designated date, in the middle of the night, and the next morning it was live. In the weeks prior to the switch, every school classroom was provided a demonstrator dial telephone for teaching purposes. I remember it being simple and natural to get the hang of. A snap. Older folks complained that all the old numbers they had memorized were now worth nothing; plus for some, the dialing process was slow and confusing. Just like now—if you have trouble with the new technology, ask your five-year-old grandchild!

Harvey Drawdy

Friends Part 1

Living on Greenway Drive during those early years as a Darlington resident turned out to be a really good thing. We stayed in Dr. Wilson's house for the first three years, then moved to another house on Greenway Drive, and were there until we left Greenway Drive in 1967. We developed great friendships while on Greenway Drive. Following is a list of people and events that I remember while living in this great neighborhood.

Bruce and Margie Lynch

Bruce and Margie were our next-door neighbors. Bruce was the shop teacher at St. John's High School. He was also the JV football coach. I was given an opportunity to help coach JV football. Working with Bruce and E. B. Davis and all the fine young men was a joy for me. Not to mention that it added an additional $100 to my annual salary. At that time of my life, I would have done it for a cap and a whistle. I remember there were several boys from Greenway Drive on our team. I am sure there may have been more, but the ones I remember and are listed on some old 1959 notes I discovered included Ingram Truluck, Billy Cain, and Andy Sansbury. The team had a winning season. Most of the boys on that team grew into fine young men and were very successful in their lives. I would have really enjoyed a career in coaching, and that was my plan…but sometimes God's plan and our plans don't mesh. When that happens…God controls the outcome!

Robert and Mary Mills

Robert, Mary, and their daughter Robin lived across the street and two houses to the left of us. Robert served in the Marine Corps during World War Two. He was actually stationed at Pearl Harbor when the Japanese attacked the US Naval base there. Robert was also a hunter and fisherman, and loved the outdoors, like me; so it is no wonder that the two of us hit it off well. We spent many mornings and afternoons over the next few years hunting and fishing together. Here are some of the many adventures and tales that I remember from our encounters with Mother Nature.

Robert and the Rattlesnakes

Robert shared with me that he had been bitten by a rattlesnake when he was a young boy, living in Cheraw, South Carolina. He and a friend were turkey hunting when they noticed a huge gobbler foraging along the banks of the river, just in range of his trusty old shotgun. Robert took dead aim and shot the turkey, and the turkey began spinning and flopping along the ground near the river. Afraid that the wounded turkey might flop into the river, Robert took off running toward the turkey. The weather was warm; so, of course, Robert was barefoot, as was the custom that time of year in the deep South. The only thing between Robert and the wounded turkey was a fallen tree which Robert hurdled with ease. As his first foot hit the ground, he felt needles penetrating his foot. He had landed on top of a rather big rattlesnake, and the snake bit him right on the top of his foot. Neither of the boys had anything suitable for a tourniquet. Robert's friend discovered a piece of baling wire on an old nearby fence and wrapped it firmly around his ankle just above the snakebite. Once he made it back home, the family rushed Robert to the nearest doctor's office. By the time they got to the doctor's office, the foot had swollen so big that it covered up the baling wire. The doctor had to cut through skin to get to the wire and then had to cut the wire off. He was told by the doctor he came close to losing the foot and that the snakebite was not as bad as the wire tourniquet that he had put on the leg to stop the flow of poison. Soon, Robert recovered from the bite; but from that day forward, he had a terrible phobia of snakes, especially rattlesnakes.

Robert Killed the Dead Snake

Robert and I decided to go squirrel hunting at the Pee Dee River Swamp. It was a nice fall day, and we knew the squirrels would be moving and feeding. Once we got to our hunting spot, Robert declared that he was going to hunt down the side of the little swamp lake, and I said I would hunt up on the hickory ridge. I felt like the squirrels would be feeding on the nuts. As I made my way over to the hickory grove, I stepped over a log, and it felt like a hammer had hit me on the bottom of my right foot. I knew exactly what had happened—a snake, and by the feel of it, he was a big one. I jumped back as the snake coiled to strike again. I gave him a mouthful of twelve-gauge pellets. It blew his head slam off his body. As I stepped around the dead snake, my intentions were to continue my hunt, but who could look for squirrels in trees when there were snakes on the ground? Soon I gave up hunting and decided to go back to the truck and wait on Robert. Along the way, I picked up that rattler by the tail and dragged him out with me. As I came out of the woods, the devil must have jumped on my back, because that's when I had the thought to have a little fun with Robert and this dead snake. I knew the path that Robert would be following out of the woods, so I coiled that dead snake up on the path and dragged a log onto the path in front of the snake. When Robert steps over the log, he will step right on the snake's back. I hustled back to the truck and waited. Soon I heard Robert coming down the trail when all of a sudden I heard a bloodcurdling scream, the unloading of both barrels of Robert's twelve-gauge shotgun, and then a string of four-letter words fit for a sailor. When Robert got to the truck, he was as pale as a sheet. He told me about the giant rattlesnake that he stepped on and the miracle that he didn't get bitten by the snake. It was right at this point that I realized the error of my ways, and that's when I made an executive decision to never tell my good friend about the dead-snake prank. And if my ole hunting buddy were still alive today…this story would have been omitted!

Are We Gonna Fish or Swim?

Coach Jimmy Welch owned a fishing cabin on the Little Pee Dee River, at a place called "White Oak." The Little Pee Dee had the reputation for "redbreast" fishing. Redbreasts are a type of bream that generally feed on the bottom; and when you hook one, hold on—they can really give you a fight. Coach Welch said we could go fishing at his place anytime we wanted to and could even use his boat that he kept chained up to a big ole cypress tree near the bank of the river. One day, Robert and I were talking, and we had heard rumors that the redbreasts were tearing it up on the Little Pee Dee. We decided to go give 'em a try. Robert checked with Coach, and he gave us the go-ahead. We had a bucket of crawfish for bait, Robert's five-horse Mercury motor, a boat chained up at the river, and the expectations of catching our limit of big ole redbreasts.

When we arrived at the river cabin, the river was higher than normal, almost at flood stage. The boat was chained to a tree, a good three or four feet from the water's edge due to the high water level. Robert said that wasn't a problem. He knew where Coach hid the boat key, so he retrieved it and then walked down to the edge of the river. He said, "Harvey, I'll jump over into the boat, unlock it, then paddle over to you. Then we can load up the boat." Sounded like a good plan to me! Robert backed up, got a little running start, and leaped toward the boat. Then he landed on one foot in the boat before making a perfect dive right into the river on the far side of the wooden boat. My thought was, *Are we gonna fish or swim?* Robert then surfaced, looked at me, and shouted, "There's the biggest damn snake in the boat that I have ever seen!" He then unlocked the boat, pulled it to shore, and killed the snake; then we went fishing!

Robert's Unsinkable Boat

Back in the day, most small fishing boats were handmade out of wood. Cypress wood was kind of the top of the line. Most of us that fished a lot wanted to have at least a small two-man boat or canoe to fish out of. As a teacher with a family, I had to work two jobs to make ends meet. My second job was with the recreation department. That's when Harmon Baldwin and I became good friends. At some point, Harmon and I decided to build our own two-man boat. We recruited Bruce Lynch, the shop teacher at the high school, to help us and to let us build it in his shop at nights when no students were there. We spent many nights there building, sanding, and painting that boat. It turned out better than we thought it would. We had a five-horsepower Elgin motor to propel the boat. I also built a rack for the top of my '55 Chevy and carried that boat on top of my car most of the summer. That way, if Harmon and I ever had a little bit of free time, we could be at the river or lake in a short period of time.

Another option for boat builders was "boat kits." That brings me to Robert's unsinkable boat. He ordered it out of a magazine that billed it as unsinkable. Now Robert had his own shop behind his house and tools to do the work. He spent many nights working on his boat, and soon it was ready. The next Saturday, a fine group of redbreast fishing experts set out for Coach Welch's river cabin at White Oak on the Little Pee Dee River in Gresham, South Carolina. There were six of us on this adventure and the christening of the *Roberto Unsinkable Boat*. Robert and Harmon were going to fish from the unsinkable boat, Cotton James and Orvell Anderson from their johnboat, and EB Davis and I were in the boat that Harmon and I had built. We finally got all the boats in the water and all the men in the boats; and we set out for a special sandbar that Robert knew about—one that was guaranteed to produce all the redbreast bream that we could legally carry home with us. Robert was leading the way in the unsinkable boat, and EB and I were lagging way behind. EB was a big man at 280 pounds, and I weighed in at 220, so my little boat and five-horsepower were doing all they could do. In addition, the boat was sitting so low in the water that I was afraid we might flip over.

About that time, I saw the two boats ahead of us side by side as if they were talking, and then Robert whipped his new boat around and headed straight for me and EB. As he got close, he yelled for us to step on the gas…that we had a long way to go to the special fishing spot. So I opened it wide open just as Robert's boat passed me, and a huge wave was created that went right over the bow of Robert's boat. It drove his unsinkable boat straight to the bottom of the Little Pee Dee River. When I turned around, all I could see was Robert and Harmon standing up in the middle of the river, up to their necks in water. All of their gear was floating downstream. Orval and Cotton were upstream, laughing, EB and I were gathering anything floating that we could get to, and Harmon and Robert were trying to get the boat up and to the bank to empty it. We finally got everything straight and got them back in the boat and, eventually, made it to the sandbar where we fished and laughed and argued with Robert all day. He has never admitted that his boat sank; he claimed that the motor was too powerful and it drove the front of the boat down. But the five of us who witnessed it sinking never stopped ribbing him about his unsinkable boat!

Robert, Mary, and Robin Mills remained close friends for many years, even after we moved away from Greenway Drive. Merle, Stan, Ricky, and I enjoyed many beach camping trips to Lake Arrowhead with the Mills family. Years later, Mary passed away, and Robin moved away and wound up with a good job in government. Robert and I remained close friends until his death several years ago. He was in his late nineties. I will always remember those good times we had hunting, fishing, and camping. A man is truly blessed to have good friends, and I was blessed to know and love Robert and his family.

Coach Jimmy Welch

I became friends with Coach Jimmy Welch in 1958. It was our first year in Darlington, and he was the football coach and athletic director at the high school. He hired me to help Coach JV football, JV basketball, and JV baseball. Coach Welch was a quail hunter and did not hunt much in the Pee Dee swamp. Robert Mills talked him into going squirrel hunting with us in Brockington Hunting Club. Somehow, Coach had wandered away from me and Robert and had gotten lost. When we found him, he was soaking wet and all scratched up from walking through the thick brush and bamboo. He had walked from the club down the river all the way to Lowder's Lake.

Coach was also part of the men's club that met once a month at Mineral Springs, where we shared a meal of wild game or fish. Fenny Baldwin was always the cook, and the menu was always wild game or fish. Fenny was Harmon's dad and was a great cook. I believe he could make an old leather shoe taste good if he wanted to. One night, the menu was squirrel stew, and I was providing the meat. I had a sack of squirrels and had also killed two young raccoons. I told Fenny about the coons, and he said clean them and bring them to me with the squirrels. I carried the game to him that morning; and when he got to Mineral Springs that night, he had squirrel stew, rice, and what he called "mystery meat." He had cut up those two coons into small chunks of meat, battered it in his secret herbs and spices, and then fried it in a pressure cooker to crispy golden-brown nuggets. Everyone was talking about how good the nuggets of mystery meat were, and we were guessing what it might be. All sorts of possibilities were mentioned. Then Coach Welch said he didn't care what it was as long as it wasn't coon. He went on to say that he would never eat a coon no matter how hungry he was. When Fenny told that the mystery meat was coon, Coach shook his head and said that he had been missing out all his life because that coon was the best meat he ever tasted.

Coach Welch was not only a great coach; he was a good man. He always looked out for me; I guess he knew it was a struggle to raise a family on a teacher's salary alone. He gave me extra money to help with the JV teams, and when I gave up coaching, he hired me to be the gatekeeper at all home games and paid me a supplement for that. Coach was also in with the Darlington Raceway owners, and he always found a job for me during the races. He was a good friend.

Fran Wall Weaver

Our Neighborhood Part 1

Mr. Cain

When returning to the Greenway Driveway neighborhood in 1957, Bimmy and I quickly renewed our friendship from the days of riding our hobby horse his dad helped assemble on Christmas Eve 1954. One day, the two of us set out on a little stroll down Evans toward Spring Street (OFF-LIMITS). We passed the Scotts' home, their open field, and came to a very pretty wooded area on our left. We were thrilled to find a host of beautiful daffodils/jonquils on the edge of the road by the marshland ditch. We began to harvest—all of them. Our arms were full of flowers making beautiful bouquets to be presented to our mothers. Thelma Wall and Noni Bonnoitt were on the phone with each other within minutes and "stroking out" over us stealing Bill Cain's roadside flowers. Within minutes, our mothers escorted Bimmy and me up to the Cains' house, to give back the prize we had collected as well as apologizing for being thieves! Our heads hung low, so you can imagine our surprise when Mr. Cain gifted the flowers right back to us! Our mothers could keep their bouquets, and we were Proud as Punch. I was a bit surprised when Mr. Cain asked if I would be an Office Proctor once I entered St. John's High School; hence, he really had forgiven me! (You see it is better to give than to receive.)

Car Pool

Between our first family stay on Greenway Drive in 1954 and our second move to Evans Circle in 1957, Mother had just gotten her driver's license. She had taken her driving test in our 1956 Country Squire station wagon that my father had ordered while stationed in Japan. The wagon was made in Detroit at a cost of $2,600 and was a beautiful blue color with wood side panels. It was a perfect size for my dad to drive since he was well over six feet tall, but my mother was "tiny" and a bit lost behind the wheel.

Our arrival on Evans offered Mother the opportunity to take a turn in a car pool. We teamed up with the Sansburys, since Clevie, Andy, and I attended Miss Cook's Kindergarten. Mother, being a bit nervous while driving, would speak over her right shoulder to us in the backseat, often telling us to "Sit Down and Be Quiet!" Andy always wanted to climb over the backseat, into the cargo area. That is where he rode in his family station wagon. The four Sansbury kids competed for the far back right side of their station wagon cargo area because Mary Anne could not reach there to smack them with her flip-flop when they misbehaved. Well, on our trip to kindergarten that day, Andy took the liberty of going right over our backseat into the coveted cargo area. Mother had crossed over Cashua Street and was making her way to Miss Cook's on little side streets. She took a left turn at the exact time Andy was coming out of the cargo area and climbing over into the backseat to be with Clevie and me again. Oh dear, as we turned, he stepped on the door handle; and *poof,* he ejected right out of the car, landing on the sandy dirt road. Vanished! Gone! Clevie and I were trying to alert Mama about the mishap all while she was telling us to "Sit Down and Be Quiet!" We went a full block before she understood Andy was no longer with us. Lo and behold, poor Mother had to return him to Mary Anne all scared, with road rash and bleeding.

Going to See Santa Claus

When Barbara and I were in kindergarten, her dad, Coach Jimmy Welch, took us to Sears in Florence to see Santa. Now this was a big deal—seeing Santa was great, but Sears also had lots of toys on display. I don't know if pretty, sweet Belva assigned this outing to Coach or if he had some item he needed to pick up. Maybe he wanted to see Santa too! We rode in his medium-size station wagon, positioned right beside him, and were so excited we scooted up to the edge of the front seat, put our hands on the dashboard, and sang Christmas songs to the top of our lungs the entire trip. Poor Coach must have had a migraine by the time we arrived. I AM sure we affected his hearing!

Barbara Welch's Wrecks

On Greenway Drive, where the creek flows under the road, my special friend Barbara was riding along on her big-girl bike when out of nowhere one of Jimmy Brown's bird dogs (Francis) ran right smack in front of her. When the two collided, Barbara flew right over her handlebars, landed on the rocky asphalt road, and was completely knocked out cold (those nasty asphalt roads liked to scrape the skin off us often). Vera and I were shocked, wide-eyed with our mouths wide open and scared to death. Once we came to our senses, one of us raced to get Belva while the other stood guard by Barbara and paced. Thank heavens she came to and lived! I am not sure about the dog. Get this—Coach Welch had two bird dogs: one, a pointer named Bell, after Belva; and the other, a setter named Lynn, after Barbara Lynn Welch. Belva and Barbara had namesakes. See how much Coach loved his girls!

Now Barbara did not just have a dog wreck; she also had a severe car wreck. Vera and I were along for the ride; and, oh, dear, while we were turning around in the median of the road on the Florence Highway, we were hit from behind. This knocked our car's backseat loose and pushed Vera into the floorboard. Someone appeared telling us to get out of the car and to get to the side of the road. As soon as we got out, a second vehicle hit us, this time on the right front side of our car. This collision pushed Barbara's car right into Barbara, taking her to the ground. She was a bit rattled (almost knocked out), and she screamed as she thought the car was on top of her. It took us a bit of time to get ourselves collected. This occurrence greatly outranked the Dog Wreck! (All those years of crossing the creek between our houses produced a sweet, precious lifelong friendship for Barbara and me.)

Stan Drawdy

That Dad-Gummed Racing Movie

O ne of the great things about living on Greenway Drive was that it was in Darlington, South Carolina. Darlington is the home of NASCAR. The Darlington Raceway was the first track of its kind anywhere in the world. It is *The Granddaddy of Them All*. And because Darlington is a famous place, lots of famous people come here; and when they come here, ordinary folks, like those of us on Greenway Drive, might get to see them. Sometimes, we may even get to get an autograph or a picture. Every year at the Southern 500 parade, some famous movie star would show up and would be the grand pooh-bah of the parade. Matt Dillon from *Gunsmoke*, and Doc and Festus, and Clint Eastwood (Rowdy Yates) from *Rawhide* were just a few of the celebs who were in the parade. I would say that the racetrack brought a lot of famous folks to our quaint little town. Maybe that's one of the reasons it is affectionately called "the Pearl of the Pee Dee."

That brings me to that dad-gummed racing movie. One time, a film crew and movie production company came to town to make a movie about racing. A major portion of the movie was filmed in and around Darlington and the raceway. The title of the movie is *Thunder in Carolina*, starring Rory Calhoun. He was pretty popular because he was in a lot of the Western movies of the day, and even starred with Marilyn Monroe in a movie about the *River of No Return*. Rory played a racecar driver who got started by outrunning cops while transporting bootleg whiskey. The pit crew chief consisted of a one-armed mechanic (the skipper from Gilligan's Island) and, of course, some pretty girl actresses. I never saw the movie, but you can still see it on Prime or one of those internet TV networks. Anyway, part of the movie was filmed near Greenway Drive. If you crossed the dam behind the Dewitts' house and followed the path toward and beside Mrs. Muldrow's house and then crossed over Main Street, one of those houses had a mechanic's garage in the back, and the crew was filming some scenes there. And the word was that you could watch and maybe get autographs. And everyone knows that if you get a famous autograph and keep it safe for a hundred years or so, then you might become rich one day.

I am basing all this on what my good friend, Johnny, had said! So we decided to go watch some celebs and get some autographs and save them till we got old. Well, ever heard of "A day late and a dollar short"? That is what we were. We got there, and a racecar was there, but there were no movie stars and no film crew. There were a couple of men there, and they told us that they had finished filming there the day before. We told the men we had come to get some autographs. One of the guys reached in his pocket and pulled out two small, flat square pieces of metal and handed each of us one. Then he told us that it was a piece of the car that was used in the movie and that they were handing them out as souvenirs instead of autographs. We left a bit discouraged, and on the way home, Johnny said that the small piece of metal was "bull crap." As we walked across the dam, he took his piece of "bull crap" and threw it into the pond. I took mine out of my pocket and drop-kicked it as far as I could, right out into the middle of Dewitts' Pond. No one cares about that dad-gummed racing movie, anyway.

Ingram Truluck

The Legend of
Whirlpool Jackson

Whirlpool Jackson was famous to the boys of Greenway Drive. Why? Because we never could catch him! He was the biggest redbreast that lived in Dewitts' Pond, and we were dying to bring him in. We wanted many things: to have the bragging rights for catching the largest fish in our world, to prove to ourselves that it could be done with a cane pole and a bread ball on a tiny hook, but most of all to stop Whirlpool from laughing at us every time we thought we had him and didn't. It was maddening!

If determination could have caught a fish, he would have been caught long ago. I was determined to be the one to catch him, hoping to beat out all the other boys who were also aware of this creature who seemed to be much smarter than us. We would occasionally think we had him hooked but would bring up a measly ordinary bream instead. Measly ordinary bream might have made some people happy but not us who knew Whirlpool Jackson, who had briefly hooked him, only to see him spit out the hook when we got him to the surface. That is when he earned his name (and I don't know who came up with it). He would look us right in the eye, then flip around and head back for the deep water, leaving a whirlpool in his wake. I imagined that he went back to his friends down below and told them about the creatures up top who thought they could catch him. But all we did was feed him bread ball after bread ball. He had it good. We had it bad. We were glad we weren't wasting worms on him. Bread was very plentiful.

One day, I was in our front yard, doing what I truly didn't want to be doing—raking pine straw into piles. I was under orders from headquarters to get the yard raked, or else! I knew what "or else" meant, and I was complying but not with any pleasure. Whirlpool Jackson never had to do any chores. I was sure of that. About that time, I looked up, and Billy Cain was walking by the house, carrying a fishing pole and a bucket. His very walk was triumphant. He was strutting along and grinning from ear to ear.

"Come look! I caught Whirlpool!" What? Billy had done it? Caught our favorite enemy, Whirlpool Jackson? But I wasn't jealous or mad at Billy. I was excited because I could finally see the fish that we had only gotten glimpses of as he teased and laughed at us. Billy proudly showed me the bucket which was nearly full of pond water. He reached in and pulled Whirlpool out. There he was! Caught forever. He wasn't laughing now but looked like an ordinary good-sized redbreast. I realize now that he was only seven or eight inches long, but that was large compared to the measly fish that we usually caught. I didn't catch him, but at least now I could rest from always trying. Suddenly, fishing in Dewitts' Pond didn't seem like such an important thing to do anymore.

Whirlpool Jackson was supper for the Cain family that night, not the Truluck family. Oh, well...

Robin Mills

Memories of Greenway Drive

L ove the Greenway Drive Project! Here's my submission. One of my favorite memories is watching Stan Drawdy's mother dancing around her house while she was cleaning and listening to Elvis and we were all running wild! She was such a joy! As Garrison Keillor was so fond of saying, "Lake Wobegon, where all the women are strong, all the men are good-looking, and all the children are above average!" It could be said of Greenway Drive in the '50s and '60s. Was it idyllic? Yes, in many ways. The memories of playing from daylight till dark, catching fireflies, having the freedom from fear, which enables one to drink in nature and take chances to try things like sliding down the metal roofs of barns onto bales of hay, to build "houses" of boughs from pine trees, to fish in our local ponds and streams—were rare and precious things. Of course, there were tough times too. There weren't as many girls as boys, and we were treated roughly…from not being allowed to go into the boys' tree houses to having to accept being the Indians instead of the cowboys in games of cowboys and Indians.

However, I truly believe that made me tougher and able to compete without fear in the adult workforce as an equal. The purest and most beautiful memories were of the friendships…between not only the children but their parents. There were many summer evenings when the "lawn chairs" would be pulled out by the parents in groups, and they would talk and laugh while the kids ate watermelon and chased fireflies and played with the many dogs who roamed freely in the neighborhood. We were each "everyone's child." We knew any parent witnessing bad behavior had the right and responsibility to discipline the offender. That neighborhood was special but made so by many very special parents who loved and cared for all of us. I count myself to be so blessed to have had loving, kind, and generous parents, and to have had so many caring and loving and generous neighbors.

Keith Carter

Visits with Jimbo and Kal-el

When Jimbo Brown was a kid, he was known as Jimmy. With some age, he changed to Jim. At some point in high school, he became Jimbo. I knew his middle name was Belvin, and I sometimes called him that, which, of course, he didn't like. While growing up, from birth until our family moved away from Greenway Drive when I turned nine years old, he and I were pretty good buds. I went to his house very often during those years, and we always had good times.

We both liked to draw. His dad had a drafting table in one room, and he always had lots of paper and pencils, and Jimmy's big thing was tracing characters out of comic books, so we did that together. It was good training in learning how to draw, which we both wanted to get better at. We both loved *Superman* and *Superboy* comic books, and we would trace many drawings out of them, learning a little each time. Almost everyone knows about Superman and his alter ego, Clark Kent. *Superman* became very popular during the baby boom years, with kids all over the country and world buying the comic books. Lesser known was the younger version of Superman—Superboy—but to us he was equally fantastic. The comic books would come out monthly, and we tried not to miss any when they showed up at Rose's dime store. Back then they cost a dime.

The story of Superman was this: he was born on the planet Krypton, and his parents learned that their planet was doomed to be destroyed by a huge asteroid. The parents wanted to preserve the life of their baby boy, Kal-el, so they got a spaceship and rigged it up for Kal-el to escape to Planet Earth before their world was destroyed.

96

They packed him into the rocket with baby bottles, blankets, and such, and told him goodbye. Just before Krypton was destroyed, Kal-el was blasted into space, pointed toward Earth. The rocket made it and crash-landed in a field in Kansas or some such state, and of course, baby Kal-el was unhurt. An elderly farm couple, Ma and Pa Kent, were driving to town (Smallville) one day and happened upon the rocket that had crashed beside the road. They stopped to investigate and found a baby inside, safe and sound. They figured out that the baby must have come from outer space; and therefore, finders, keepers. They took him in, named him Clark, and raised him as their own since they didn't have any children. They discovered the baby's superpowers when they were on the way to town one day and had a flat tire. (It turned out that Kryptonians had superpowers on Earth—well, Kal-el was the only one who made it.) While Pa Kent was fumbling around in the trunk for the jack, toddler Clark went to the front of the car and lifted it up like it weighed nothing. Ma and Pa were astounded, of course, but Pa gladly changed the tire, and they kept the secret to themselves. Little Clark (Superbaby) came in very handy around the farm as he grew up, being able to lift anything that needed lifting. He could also boil a pot of water just by staring at it.

Clark Kent became a handsome teenager and filled out into a muscular young fellow. He liked nothing better than to do good deeds, rescue people, and defeat the bad guys while flying around dressed as Superboy. Besides being able to fly and being superstrong, he had X-ray vision, could melt steel with his eyes, and bullets would just bounce off of him. It wasn't always easy to keep his superpowers a secret as he was growing up and going to school, etc. Despite his superpowers and good looks, he was always very humble and shy. Girls, of course, loved him, but Clark acted like he didn't have the slightest idea about any of that.

Eventually, as Clark matured into a man, Ma and Pa Kent died, and Clark moved to Metropolis. He became a reporter and worked for *The Daily Planet* newspaper, which allowed him to stay up on the news, since in his secret life he was Superman and it helped him get a jump on emergency situations. He wore his skintight blue leotard and red cape under his dress clothes; and when his services were needed, he would sneak away (usually into a phone booth), take off his glasses, tear off his dress clothes, and fly away to do good deeds. He had to really work to keep his super identity a secret from his coworker girlfriend, Lois Lane, and everybody else. Lois always wondered why Clark was absent when Superman was punishing the bad guys, but she never seemed to catch on. It was funny since Superman didn't wear a mask or anything to disguise his looks, except not wear his usual nerdy glasses.

The only thing that could hurt Superman was kryptonite. Kryptonite was a part of the Planet Krypton that had blown up and just happened to be available to mean guys. Being near a chunk of kryptonite drained Superman of his powers, and it would kill him if he was around it for long. His enemies, especially Lex Luthor, knew about this and managed to use kryptonite to put Superman out of commission when they could, allowing them to do their evil deeds and hopefully kill him. But he always got out of each bind and came back to knock them out, tie them up, and leave them for the police to haul in, taking zero credit for anything, ever.

This is what Jimmy and I spent a lot of time reading, tracing, and discussing. Each issue of the comic book had a letter or two from readers that asked questions about Superman/boy/baby. I decided to write in to ask who sewed back all the shirt buttons that Clark Kent popped off every time he ripped off his clothes, revealing his Superman outfit. The buttons would just fly off and go everywhere. But the next time, his shirts were just like new. My letter was published in a later issue! The answer was a bit lame, saying that Ma Kent must have always had a lot of buttons to sew back on constantly. But Ma Kent was dead! Somebody else had to sew them back on, unless Clark bought new shirts every day. Jimmy nor I could believe that my letter made the comic book. I was too dumb to think of saving that issue for proof—it didn't cross my mind. At that age, whatever happened was normal. Jimbo reminded me of the Superman letter at our fortieth high school reunion, which I had forgotten about, so confirm it with him if you don't believe me!

We eagerly acquired and read other comic books too: *Batman*, *The Flash*, *Spiderman*, *Aquaman*, *Green Lantern*, and *The Blackhawks*, to name a few. *The Blackhawks* are unknown now but were a squad of about seven jet pilots who flew the coolest black fighter jets. Each guy was of a different nationality; and each of their nearly identical jets had some special feature that the others didn't have, that provided them diverse ways of defeating the enemy fighters; one jet, for example, had a giant crossbow that shot large arrows. The common denominator among all the comic books we read was that evil was always being evil, and the good guys always fought them and won. We knew it was fantasy, but it was wholesome and positive. I think it did us good. After all, our dads had fought the Japs and the Krauts and won! We expected it—it was normal.

The Browns took *National Geographic*. Jimmy and I read them out on the side screen porch for privacy. Almost every issue had the obligatory photos of Africans in their native outfits. In the ladies' case, it was always with nothing on from the waist up. We were astounded on a regular basis. "Look at this one!" "Wow!" It was an education. Did we learn any geography? Nope.

Jimmy's sister, Robbie, was several years older than him. She seemed to be out most of the time when I was there (shock, shock). I remember Jimmy taking me to her room to play with her 8-Ball (a no-no if she had been there). Some would know that this was like an oversized black billiard ball, was filled with water, and had a little round window on the bottom. You (well, girls) were supposed to ask a question out loud to the 8-Ball and then turn it over and watch as a white shape would float up to the window, showing a short answer to the question. It was sort of like opening a fortune cookie. It was interesting to try to see all the different answers that were in there. Robbie had a record player and plenty of 45s, but the only three songs we cared about were "Hound Dog," "Purple People Eater," and "The Witch Doctor." The Witch Doctor in the song said (sang) only one thing: "Ooo-eee oo-ah-ah, ting tang, walla-walla bing-bang" (repeat). This was so catchy that we would go around the rest of the day singing it. No wonder Robbie was always out.

Jimmy's mother regularly bought angel food cake, wrapped in cellophane. Anytime we got hungry, and many times when we weren't, Jimmy and I went to the pantry where he got out the latest angel food cake and unwrapped it. We broke off chunks of it and ate it—no plate, no fork, no napkin, no problem. With its golden-brown exterior and almost-white interior, Jimmy named it "Rotten Cotton." Every time I went for a visit, getting some rotten cotton was standard fare. His mother apparently bought it just for us, and I don't ever remember her saying a word about us clawing off hunks of it until it was all gone.

Now you see why I enjoyed going to visit Jimmy/Jimbo!

Boys and Bicycle Tricks

On Greenway Drive, we rode bikes a lot. We had bicycle races that were amazingly organized by Ingram Truluck and Leonard Ballard, our neighborhood ringleaders, but what I want to recall are the stunts we did on bicycles. Bicycles were for getting places quickly, but ordinary riding was pretty humdrum, so we found ways to turn bike riding into entertainment.

We started pretty tamely; we would slide backward off the seat onto the back fender (or onto the flat "seat" over the back tire) and pedal along in that stretched-out position. That was pretty lame after a bit, so we began standing on the seat while we coasted, then on one foot with the other leg stretched way back. We had the secret idea that it would amaze the girl population of the Drive. I (once) tried standing on the seat and letting go of the handlebars, but the front wheel immediately went berserk, and I came crashing down in a heap.

It wasn't long before someone (like Ingram) had the great idea of making jumping ramps for our bikes. We used Evans Street because it was not paved and thus more forgiving than Greenway. Plus it ran slightly downhill which helped as we worked on our bicycle stunts. For the ramp, we took a wooden plank a few feet long and put some bricks under the downhill end of it. We pedaled hard down the hill and over the ramp. We discovered that speed was our friend—going slow was a recipe for nothingness, even for wiping out in slo-mo. The faster we went, the more stable the jump was, and of course, it allowed us to fly further past the ramp. This inevitably led to seeing who could jump the farthest, so one boy would mark the point of touchdown with a stick and then measure the distance and record it in a notebook. The competition led to more speed, more distance, and more accidents. If we landed with the front wheel angled the least bit, we would go kerflooey. Torn pants with skinned knees (shorts were for sissies) and skinned elbows were our red badges of courage.

One of the downsides to the ramp-jumping was the damage to handlebars. We would jerk up on the handlebars as we hit the end of the ramp to get more distance, but when we landed, our weight would come down on the handgrips, and eventually, the handlebars bent downward. We would bend them back straight, but then they were weakened. I remember jumping with my little bike, and one wounded handlebar broke clean off when I landed. This caused me to lose control and wipe out very thoroughly. All of this pointed out our wisdom of ramp-jumping on a dirt street. Wipeouts would have been brutal on pavement.

We began adding extra daring and intrigue to our ramp-jumping. We big boys (I was seven or eight at the time) offered for some of the little boy bystanders (like Andy and Danny Sansbury) to lie on the ground at the end of the ramp so we could jump over them. We knew how far we could jump due to our practice, so the width of two boys was nothing; we cleared them with room to spare. We put out a call for more bodies (even girls), but volunteers were slow stepping up. So we instituted a draft, and to show the onlookers that being jumped over by a boy on a bicycle wasn't dangerous, we took our turns under the jumpers to prove it. I remember looking at the undersides of wheels, sprockets, and riders going over from that perspective, all with zero mishaps. I think Johnny Truluck, Punk, and Bimmy took their turns as jump fodder. Mothers were not helicopter parents back then, and our boy-jumping went on for a bit until Nonie Bonnoitt and Mary Anne Sansbury discovered what was going on between their houses and discouraged the practice by threatening to skin us alive.

When the thrill of ordinary ramp-jumping wore off, we moved on to other exploits with more pizzazz. We had seen one too many circus acts on TV or in comic books, I guess, so we built a rectangular wooden frame just past the ramp that we could jump through. After a few jumps to make sure it was both high and wide enough for a boy and a bicycle, we covered the frame with newspaper using Scotch tape. The frame was placed a few feet past the end of the ramp; and the boy with the most seniority (which was always Ingram) got to race down the street on his bike, hit the ramp, and burst triumphantly through the newspaper before landing. We went through several days' worth of newspapers and a lot of tape in a hurry, which became tiresome. But we weren't finished. Next?

Remember the two primal things that boys are attracted to? Fire and water. We had a creek and ponds just down the street which provided our water fix, so this called for fire. We wrapped the wood frame in rags, poured kerosene over the rags, and struck a match, creating a rectangle of fire to jump through. The good thing was, we could do repeated jumps with the fire frame, unlike the labor-intensive, one-and-done newspaper trick. And this was very safe! We were moving so fast on our bikes that we couldn't get burned, even if we touched the fire. We took turns jumping through the burning ring of fire until the frame finally burned up.

No video games for us back in the day!

Stan Drawdy

The Sanctuary

Sanctuary is defined as a place of refuge or safety, a place that provides protection from danger or difficult situations. Greenway Drive had such a place, and many of us kids occasionally took advantage of our very own safe space. Our neighborhood sanctuary was the Sansburys' yard, or 107 Greenway Drive.

The Sansbury family was great. Paul, the father, was an attorney; and his wife, Mary Anne, was like a second mom to many of us. She often invited us kids in for Rice Krispies Treats or to watch the *Wonderful World of Color* on their color TV. I think they were the first family on Greenway Drive to have a color television. She also was the first to put a layer of chocolate on top of the Rice Krispies Treats (so good)! During the summers, she would sometimes take me with her family to Black Creek swimming and taught me to swing out over the creek on a tree rope and drop into the dark, cool water. Mrs. Sansbury was so awesome, and she spent a lot of time with her kids and with many of us other kids too.

Her kids were Clevie, the oldest daughter, and then Andy, the oldest son. Andy was a year older than me. Then came Danny, the youngest son; and the caboose was Susie. Like I said, they were a great family. They had a great house with a huge front yard that was perfect for Wiffle ball and football. They also owned the lot beside their house that was wooded and sloped down to the stream coming out of Kilgos' Pond. Not only was their yard good for Wiffle ball and football, it was also the place where many of us kids were introduced to croquet. They would set the game up and let us play with them.

But the greatest thing about the Sansbury yard was that it was our sanctuary. No one ever told us the history of the sanctuary or how it became the sanctuary. We don't even know, to this day, why it became the sanctuary; but we all knew that the two most feared guys in the neighborhood, Punk and Bimmy Bonnoitt, would not step one foot into the Sansburys' yard.

Now don't get me wrong. Punk and Bimmy were both cool friends, and most times, I was in good graces with them both, but if they ever got angry with you for any reason, they would beat you up. But if you could just get to the Sansbury yard, you would be safe! At times, I have stood in the Sansbury yard, unable to get across the street to my house at 112 Greenway Drive because one or both of those guys were waiting on the edge of the yard, hoping I would get close enough to the edge. I know what a sea lion must have felt like stranded on an iceberg with the killer whales cruising the edges, waiting to pounce. Sometimes, I felt bad for Punk and Bimmy because we had some great games in the Sansbury yard and they would not get to play. Despite their rarely occurring mean streaks, Punk and Bimmy were great friends to have. They were tough guys and good athletes. Their dad, John, ran the ice house in Darlington; and their mom, Noni, was very nice. I remember they had a giant striped bass on the wall that everyone said Mrs. Bonnoitt had caught, but I find that hard to believe because the fish was almost as big as she was. Sandra and Linda were the older sisters. They used to babysit Rick and me occasionally. They were a lot prettier than the Bonnoitt brothers!

Once I got to really know Punk and Bimmy, they became two of my closest friends in the neighborhood and in school. Later, we played on the same football team, and today I feel that they are both close enough friends that I could call on either of them if I needed them. And I have learned that the best type of sanctuary is not a place, not a yard, not a fenced-in land. The best type of sanctuary, place of refuge, is found in the relationships that we develop within our communities, neighborhoods, and families. Greenway Drive may have had only one yard that was a sanctuary, but many relationship sanctuaries were built during our time together there, and many of them still exist today!

The Vineyard

One of my favorite memories of Greenway Drive was Mr. Cains' vineyard. Every year, his vines produced the biggest, juiciest muscadine grapes around. Mr. Cain allowed us kids, and sometimes the adults, to go into his vineyard and pick and eat all the grapes we wanted. I remember those grapes as being so sweet and juicy!

The vines had been there so long that they had actually covered about a quarter of an acre. The vines twisted up and around several posts that formed a huge rectangle. Across the top of the post was a wire screen that was covered all the way by the grapevines. The vines formed a ceiling, and the grapes were just hanging on the vines, waiting to be picked and eaten. We could stand in the shade under the vines as we enjoyed the grapes.

The vineyard was located at the back and side of the Cains' house. Mr. Bill Cain was the principal and tennis coach at St. John's High School. Mrs. Cain also taught school for many years. They had a son named Billy and a daughter named Sarah.

Mr. Cain was the principal for many years. He was a good principal and a great man. I remember that he always gave a special gift to each senior for graduation. It was a small box of a special type of candy that he actually made and packaged for each graduate. The candy was some type of apricot-flavored chewy fruity candy. I never tasted anything like it before or after I finished off my graduation box that he gave me.

I remember Mr. Cain as a very distinguished man of high moral character and very serious about his job and his school. He was a kind man who treated everyone with dignity and respect.

Two things that every kid would remember about Mr. Cain were the way he talked and his devotional at school. Mr. Cain did not speak the same way that most of us Southern kids spoke. He spoke with a very strong accent. My dad said that his accent was because he was from the Low Country of South Carolina. Mr. Cain would be responsible for the devotional only if the person assigned to do it was AWOL! Yes, we not only heard a daily Christian devotional at school, but we also prayed after the devotion was read. And we stood up, placed our right hands over our hearts, and recited the Pledge of Allegiance to the flag of the United States of America. We also prayed at all sporting events and stood for the national anthem. And we were proud of our school, our town, our state, and our country!

Sometimes, the devotion giver would fail to show up. Mr. Cain was always there to fill in, and he always read the same devotional with the accent that only he displayed. Every time, he gave the same scripture, 1 Corinthians 13:11: "When I was a child, I spoke as a child, I understood as a child, I thought as a child; but, when I became a man, I put away childish things."

Fran Wall Weaver

Our Neighborhood Part 2

Tinker Bell

My mother, Thelma Louise, had a tiny yellow parakeet with red eyes, and her name was Tinker Bell. Uncle Claud Smith raised the bird, and she was gifted at yelling out a wolf whistle and saying, "Hey, good lookin', what ya got cookin'?" Randomly, she also said, "LSMFT—Lucky Strike Means Fine Tobacco." Daily she blurted out, "Hubba, hubba, ding dang, baby you got everythang." She had a sweet little round birdcage on a stand in the dining area of our kitchen. At night, Mother put a pretty ironed white cloth over her cage—a signal for her to be quiet until morning. Tinker Bell had taken on correcting me at the table and would say, "Fran, put your napkin in your lap," "Fran, take your hand off the table," and "Fran, chew with your mouth closed." We all know where Tinker Bell learned those remarks! Mama did not have to look at me at the table anymore; therefore, Tinker Bell certainly was not my Best Bird Friend.

One day, Mother let Tinker Bell out of her cage to exercise her wings. This drill happened about once a month. Cyndie had a friend over to play when a sudden knock at the back door occurred. Mary Anne Sansbury had come to tell Mother she had just gotten sad news that her father had passed away. The back door was open while our friend, Diane Pate (a lifelong friend), was leaving with her doll bed and Mary Anne was entering. Geez Louise, next thing we knew, Tinker Bell had flown-the-coop, escaped right over our heads, out the back door, making a graceful landing in our backyard. Within the bat of an eye, Cyndie's cat pounced on the bird and chomped. Mother grabbed the broom, hit the ground running, and whopped the cat. Of course, the feisty kitty dropped poor little Tinker Bell, and in no time, Mother was on the phone with Uncle Claud receiving instructions for first aid. Tinker Bell took on a whole new persona with her red Mercurochrome-polka dotted sides.

We soon packed our clothes to go over to the Sansburys' to stay overnight while Mary Anne and Paul headed to be with her family. Us kids placed bets on the little bird's survival chances that night; and sure enough, when we uncovered little Tinker Bell's cage in the morning, she was on her back with her feet up in the air and dead as a doornail. I am ashamed to say I was not too distraught. Of course, it was time to prepare for her pet's funeral, one of many pet services held over the years. Maybe that is what prepared Danny Sansbury to become a pastor.

Swift Strike

Somewhere around 1962, our neighborhood was chosen as a site for Swift Strike exercises for the Army. Soldiers in fatigues were all over the place—in Williamson Park, at the entrance to Evans Street, in people's yards, etc. They actually had weapons with blank ammunition, and they brought tanks too. There were strict rules civilians were to adhere to. Absolutely no interaction with the soldiers, no talking to any of them, no pictures taken of them. In other words, you were to pretend they were not there. My mother did not behave as if those rules applied to her. She had us running up and down Evans, from our house to Spring Street, delivering tons of homemade hot biscuits and hot coffee. She felt having been the wife of a Marine for seventeen years qualified her to pull rank over their orders, and You Better Look Out If You Got in Her Way! Those young fellows loved her treats. Bill Brasington was not intimidated by the rules either. He took a picture of Vera, Polly, Wanda, and Billy sitting on top of one of those tanks. Bill served in the National Guard. Nothing scared him. My husband, Grady, reported to Bill when he joined the Guard, and then Bill reported to Grady after he returned from Officer's School. I am sure my dad was cheering them on. (By the way, it took all of Bill's monthly National Guard check to cover the cost of the Brasingtons' monthly-delivered-to-the-door Sealtest milk bill!)

Clevie's Photos

In 1966, Clevie became our very own fourteen-year-old neighborhood photographer. Not only did she snap photos, but believe it or not, she developed her own film! The Sansburys had an interior hall bathroom with small little green square tiles. They ran from ceiling to floor, and even the tub was made from them. There was no natural light in this area, so it became Clevie's very own dark room. I have to tell you, she was smart and always ahead of her time. I was certainly no help but privileged to witness her developing film and hanging photos to dry on her makeshift interior bathroom clothesline. Good Grief, she should have handed one of us the camera to take a picture of her. She is kindly sharing the results of her labor with you. It is true—a Picture Is Worth a Thousand Words!

Merle Drawdy

The Housewives
of Greenway Drive

Housewives and moms had lots of chores back during my Greenway Drive years. *Luxury* was not a word in the vocabulary of most of us on Greenway Drive during the 1950s and 1960s. We had the basic necessities but no extras. It was years before I even had my first washing machine. I took my laundry uptown to the Laundromat on Wednesdays. This was an all-day job! Sometimes, I would wash and dry, but if it was nice weather, I would wash only and save that money it cost to run the big dryers. Then I would take my wet clothes home and hang them out on the clothesline that Harvey put up in the backyard.

Grocery day was usually near the end of the week, and I had to plan out the meals for the entire week. Plans centered around the amount of money that we had for that week after paying all the other bills. I made out a weekly grocery list. As I shopped, I compared prices of different brands till I found the best price. Then I would check the item off my list until all items were checked off. I remember seeing some women shopping and throwing things into their buggy without having to check the price. I would think, *Wow! Would this ever be for me?* Don't get me wrong. I was not complaining because we were very blessed. We never went to bed hungry and never skipped a meal, but we had to be thrifty!

God supplied all of our needs and then some. He provided more Kool-Aid than Cokes. Cokes were a treat back then. Many of the kids in the neighborhood told me I made the best Kool-Aid. My secret ingredient was "more sugar than called for." Most of the snacks we had were homemade. Ice cream could be made in the freezer, in ice trays, using milk, sugar, and vanilla extract. I made fudge with cocoa and sugar…Stan's favorite. I made S'mores in the oven before S'mores ever had a name, but my version was a saltine cracker with peanut butter and a marshmallow browned on top. Another favorite was donuts. You can tear a hole in the center of a canned biscuit and then deep-fry it in oil till it turns brown and floats. Then top it with melted sugar or powdered sugar. I also made my own pimento cheese for sandwiches. We made our own jams and jellies, as well as canning veggies. Freezing would have been easier, but who could afford a chest freezer back in the day? You get the point. We made do with whatever we had, and we were blessed.

An air conditioner was such a luxury back then and was tops on my wish list. I have always been hot natured. Attic fans and ceiling fans helped some at night, but when we got our first AC from Sears, on the credit plan, I thought I had died and gone to heaven.

Summers were a bit brutal with the heat, the gnats, and mosquitoes. But we did find ways to have fun. The kids played in a small plastic pool in our backyard, while I worked on my tan. The only pools were privately owned except for the Country Club members' pool. We would take the kids swimming at Cheraw State Park or to the beach occasionally. One year, a group asked us to help build a community pool by becoming a charter member, and that's how the Sun 'n' Splash became a reality for many of us in Darlington. A dream come true for the kids and frankly for us moms too. When completed, it included a large community pool, tennis courts, and picnic tables with a shelter. I remember many days with Lottie and some of the other housewives and kids at the pool, picnic lunches, and just spending the day with friends relaxing. Sometimes, the dads would show up after work and bring watermelons, and we would go over to the shelter and enjoy socializing. Those were some great times! So much fun and fellowship. God is so good! We also had a great recreation department in Darlington run by Harmon Baldwin. Church softball for the men and youth baseball for the kids. Always a game to go to or some activity to get involved in. We spent many afternoons and nights at the ball fields and at the special events sponsored by the Rec department.

The things I remember most are not the scores of the games or the specifics of the events but rather the PEOPLE involved. It was a time when people seemed to really love and care about each other. God seemed to be important in the lives of most people. Church on Sunday was a given, not a maybe. We may not have had all the conveniences of modern day, but what we did have was much more fulfilling to the human spirit. We may not have had the material things that we all enjoy these days, but we had love for each other, which is more valuable than gold. We were put here to love God and to love each other. These principles were found to be alive on Greenway Drive.

Sammy L. Howell

I Won Life's
Lottery Many Times!

P lease let me explain. My good fortune began when I was born to
two wonderful and loving parents in the United States of America
in 1952. They brought me home from McLeod Hospital to a little
house on Spring Street Extension. This house was small in size but
huge in family love. Our house was built in a new housing development rising up outside of the town of Darlington, South Carolina, on
streets named Greenway Drive, Spring Street Extension, Pinehaven
Avenue, and Evans Circle. The neighborhood was built right near
Williamson Park. The park afforded young and old alike a place of
fun, adventure, beauty, and a retreat from the hustle and bustle of a
small town. Of course, it was a haven for critters like snakes and mosquitoes, and no good thing usually comes without some costs. On
the bright side, it was a great source of serpents for Ingram Truluck.
Since he was much older, I really did not know Ingram other than by
his legend as a collector of and interest in snakes. He certainly had
access to them in the creek and woods behind his Greenway Drive
home. As I grew, I found out how fortunate and blessed I was to live
in this great neighborhood. I was surrounded by kind and loving
adults that watched out for me. These streets were filled with many
friends; and together we grew, played, argued, sometimes fought,
made up, and moved on as we developed memories and friendships
that remain today.

Mine is not a specific story but more of a series of remembrances. My uncle Bill Shepard submits articles for the *News and Press* about his days growing up in Darlington on the Mill Village. Periodically, he submits a piece and asks the question, "Do You Remember When?" Perhaps you remember some of these.

I remember when:

- The neighborhood was full of Ballards, Kilgos, Stokes, Beckhams, Cains, Brasingtons, Tyners, McKelveys, Lynchs, Dewitts, Trulucks, Sansburys, Bonnoitts, Welchs, Browns, Smyres, Walls, Powers, Flowers, Drawdys, Howles, DuBoses, Smiths, Howells, Scotts, Meltons, Suggs, Ingrams, and Pates.

- The snow and ice storms would come, and schools would close. We would head to the park to slide down the slopes leading down from the park road. The trees and shrubs always posed a challenge, but there was fun to have.

- We would take our skateboards to surf the treacherous Suicide Hill located in front of Dr. Ned Hobbs' house near the end of the park road. We usually left with many scrapes, bumps, and bruises; but a successful ride was always worth the risk.

- The Suggs' Pond froze over, and Mrs. Sansbury brought a pair of ice skates for us to try. Whether they fit or not, we gave ice-skating a shot. I think it was the only time Darlington ever had an ice-skating rink.

- A big neighborhood bicycle race was held at Cynthia Smyre's house on Medford Drive. She had a perfect circular driveway, and there were quite a few entrants from Greenway Drive and Spring Street. Just like at the Darlington Raceway, a wreck occurred between two cyclists that resulted in a fight and required an intervention from Mrs. Eloise. Once she restored order out of the chaos, the race resumed. I believe I finished third and won a sack of pennies.

- We would modify our model cars and replace the interiors with size D batteries, tape them up, and roll them down

Spring Street toward the park and see who would win by rolling the farthest. Traffic was never a problem in those days.

- We would play baseball, softball, and Wiffle ball in Glenn, Greg, and Scott Suggs' yard. The competitive spirit was always present. Glenn would be a player-referee and adjust the rules as the game progressed. It was always interesting how he ruled on foul balls. His hits always seemed to land in fair territory when it was a close call.

- Some of us would walk to Spring Elementary, Brunson-Dargan Junior High, and St. John's High School. I remember walking down Greenway Drive and taking the shortcut through Mr. Dewitt's property to get over to the Dovesville Highway and on to Brunson-Dargan.

- Boy Scout Troop 504 under the outstanding leadership of Mr. Wells and later Mr. Chafee Jones would meet in the Scout Hut on Mr. Kilgo's property. These were great mentors for young boys. My girlfriend, Annie P., moved to Evans Drive when her mom married Bill Brasington. Oh, what a happy day that was! And Annie P. is still with me closing in on our forty-seventh wedding anniversary.

- Polly developed a crush on my cousin, Darrell, who lived in Florida. He would come for a visit, and usually he and Polly would get to see each other. Darrell was a good-looking lady's man. Such was the case that my mom even put on a mock wedding for them. Polly still asks about him to this day.

- Jimmy, Ronnie, and Wayne Smith were always ready for a basketball game in their backyard or a Wiffle ball game in their front yard.

- Mrs. Melton, my next-door neighbor, saw a few of us Spring Street fellows enjoying a few sour weeds that grew in her front yard. She asked, "Boys, do you know where those sour weeds came from?" "No, ma'am," we said. With a slight smile, she replied, "Well, they grow everywhere a dog pees." Not deterred, we kept on enjoying the tartness of a good sour weed chew.

- The city was preparing to install sewer lines along Spring Street. As they dug the trenches for the pipes in front of our house, they also dug up remnants of old seashells.
- The smell of freshly baked biscuits from Bobby and Judy Truluck's grandmother's kitchen would beckon me like a hungry dog looking for a treat at Mrs. Truluck's back door. This sweet lady would always have a biscuit for me.
- Spring Street was the cat mecca of the neighborhood. There always seemed to be a litter of wild kittens coming along, and my brother, Keith, loved each and every one. After Keith's passing, the cats somehow found a loving home on Greenway Drive. I have heard there is much speculation as to why the cats decided to make their move to Greenway Drive. However, as Sergeant Shultz in Hogan's Heroes was known to say, "I know nothing, nothing!"

I am still blessed to have my mother, Virginia (Jenny) Howell, with us. While age has taken its toll on her physically, she still has her wonderful spirit, and her memory is still scary sharp. She lives in the same house and neighborhood in which I was raised. I can assure you she still maintains a "neighborhood watch," so be warned! While I have lived in the upstate of South Carolina much longer than I lived in Darlington, my roots still run deep in the sandy soil of this great neighborhood and town. How great is it to return time and time again to my only Darlington home and to a place still filled with so many friends and precious memories? And I am still making more! No trip would be complete without a visit to the Dairy Bar for some Greek hotdogs and French fries, a drive along the streets bordering St. John's Elementary, Brunson-Dargan Junior High, St. John's High School, and the old baseball and football stadiums. I often walk the streets and the trails in the park and cross the wooden bridge where my mother would take me with my little boat tied to a string. We would let it float in the beautiful black water of Swift Creek. One day, I was heartbroken when the string broke, and the little boat disappeared in the dark waters. Just like the swift water took my little boat, time and distance eventually take its toll on all of us in one way or another. Remember that "Distance can ne'er divide us, nor time dull our loyal praise." Hopefully, we can always remember and, if we are lucky enough, continue to make memories in this wonderful neighborhood and town we grew up in.

Finally, I would like to dedicate these reflections with heartfelt thanks and appreciation in memory and honor of everyone that made these memories and experiences such a wonderful part of my life's journey. Yes, I know I won life's lottery many times growing up on Spring Street in Darlington, South Carolina.

Keith Carter

Growing Up on
Greenway Drive Part 2

C onstantly hunting and catching snakes was the other part of our
existence. We were all trained by Coach Ingram in the iden-
tification of all local snakes and knew how to spot any venomous
ones. I had, and I think most of us had, a book called *Snakes of North
America*, much like the bird books that some people enjoy. We were
remarkably knowledgeable about our subject at ages six and up. Every
so often, Ingram would lead us on a snake hunt down toward Swift
Creek, where we boys (and maybe some girls) would walk in a line
through the woods, side by side, looking for snakes or snake holes in
the ground. If either was spotted, we would call out, and everybody
would converge and either catch the snake or dig the hole out in
search of one. We would usually come away with several from these
hunts. Ingram's dad had some cages built for the snake collection in
their backyard, which were up off the ground a few feet, all built in
a row of hardware cloth, with a roof and a door to each cage which
could be latched. We would store the snakes there, feed them toads
or bugs, and take them out to play with them. We caught hogno-
ses, garter snakes, rat snakes, king snakes, black racers, green snakes,
corn snakes, and the occasional glass snake, which had a fragile tail
like a lizard which would break off easily and grow back. We also
caught water snakes in and around the ponds behind the Dewitt
house, which usually required us getting soaked. On several occasions, a water snake was caught, and it had just dined on a frog. Upon

being caught, the excited snake usually upchucked its lunch. One time when this happened, the frog was still alive and hopped away.

Standing: Keith Carter, Ingram Truluck, and Robert Payne.
Sitting: Johnny Truluck.

We would parade up and down the street with our snakes, letting them go into our shirts and out an armhole or a neckhole, grossing out most girls and mothers. We knew how to catch and hold them behind the head, and which ones would bite if they got a chance. We were all bitten any number of times, but it was harmless and didn't hurt. But one time my brother, Philip, caught a large king snake around the midsection, and it turned around and gave him a good bite on the hand, which bled. My mother took him to Dr. Coleman for a tetanus shot, and Dr. Coleman asked him if he had learned anything from the experience. Philip said, "Yes, sir, next time I won't catch him around the waist."

And what about 1959 when the Hollywood movie *Thunder in Carolina* was filmed in Darlington! I'll never forget going out in the front yard at night and watching and hearing the motors of the Goodyear blimp go over on Race Week. It had a light message board on the side which advertised the Labor Day parade, with actor Rory Calhoun (the star of the movie) as the grand marshal. Who else in small-town America had the Goodyear blimp hovering over their house in 1959—and Hollywood stars and celebrities each year in a parade: Clint Eastwood from *Rawhide*, James Garner from *Maverick*, James Arness (Matt Dillon) and Ken Curtis (Festus) from *Gunsmoke*, Chuck Connors—*The Rifleman*, Donna Douglas (Ellie Mae Clampett) from *The Beverly Hillbillies*, musicians Buck Owens and Marty Robbins, and many more stars that I'm forgetting? It was normal for us but still an amazing thing to have in our small town each year. The parade was great, with high school bands, beauty queens, many of the race car drivers, the Omar Imps and their Leapin' Lizzie car, which the clowns would pile on the back bumper and tip up onto its rear wheels; and it would go around in circles on the street, backfiring beautifully. Wow, was it great!

Melmac dinnerware was common; at least it was in our home. It was made of a tough plastic and was popular in the 1950s. Sometimes, when my mother had gone to the grocery store or somewhere, we would take a dinner plate, hold it vertically, and give it a mighty spin on the kitchen table. This was a good rainy-day exercise, to see who could make the plate spin the longest before it finally came to a stop. The real reason we did it was the final minutes of the spin, when the plate would be almost horizontal but still rotating, because it made the most delightfully loud *wown-wown-wown* sound as the cat died*. The noise sped up as the plate finished up until it finally stopped after a long deafening clatter. Mother would have never stood for it, and as far as I know, she never knew about that stimulating activity.

*This was when things naturally slowed to a stop, as in swinging.

There were other everyday activities that I remember enjoying. One was catching toads (there were lots of toads around our houses) and putting parachutes on them; that's right, parachuting toads. They did not volunteer, but that didn't stop us, and we were careful not to hurt them, since they might soon be needed for snake food. We borrowed a few handkerchiefs from our fathers' bedrooms and used cotton string to make the four lines to the parachute corners and a harness for the toad. Then we carefully rolled him up with the handkerchief and threw it as high up as we could. The parachute would open, and the stoic toad floated down as pretty as you please. A few times, we climbed up on the house and then threw Mr. Toad way up, giving him a wild ride. We also tied sewing thread to a leg of June bugs and then, using about three feet of thread and holding the other end, let him loose to fly around our heads in circles. Don't knock it till you've tried it!

Right before my family moved to the country in September of 1959, I realized a phase of my life was coming to an end. Some of us were playing in the street one Saturday, as usual, when a car turned onto Greenway Drive, headed toward us. We moved aside as it slowly approached; and as it got closer, we saw the driver was Leonard Ballard, all of thirteen years old, driving his dad's 1956 Pontiac! He was as proud as could be as we gaped at the sight. He stopped for effect, grinning big, and then slowly eased down the street, hoping to be seen by everybody, going to the end and turning around and coming back. I think he got in trouble for this stunt, as his dad, Oscar Ballard, had been a Darlington policeman for many years before opening the Deluxe Café on the square. But I'm sure Leo thought any punishment was worth it, and we agreed. At that moment, it seemed like the beginning of the end of an era for me, especially with moving away coming up. The thought of driving a car had been far from my eight-year-old brain, but suddenly I got a glimpse of the future. If Leo could drive a real car by himself, then we were soon to follow! We had tremendous fun in those days, and for me, it lasted only until we moved out to McIver Road on my ninth birthday. Nine years on Greenway, but I sure packed a lot into it!

Stan Drawdy

Striking It Rich

At some point during my years on Greenway Drive, one of the older boys took me under wing and became my close friend and mentor. I had always looked up to Johnny Truluck for many reasons. Not only was he one of the "coolest" guys in the neighborhood, but he was one of the best athletes in the whole town of Darlington. Football was his favorite sport, and he was really good at it. It became my favorite sport, too, so we had football as the starting point in our relationship. Johnny taught me a lot about the game of football in our sessions of playing toss and "rack the man." He taught me how to punt the football and how to kick off a tee—a tee that we made with a block of a two-by-four about four inches long and two ten-penny nails that we borrowed from my dad's shop. That tee worked great, and we thought about making a few more to sell, but we never really followed up with that idea.

Johnny also taught me that football was a game for tough people. Once, we were playing "rack the man with the ball." That's where one guy has the ball, and all the other players are chasing him to tackle (rack) him. One time, I got the ball, took off running, made a quick turn, and faked out the ones chasing me. Then out of nowhere came Jimbo, and he knocked the crap out of me. I must have started crying because Johnny came over and said, "Football is for tough guys. Never let them know what you are thinking or feeling." I'll never forget that line. It is true in football, in the business world, and life. Never let your opponents know what you are thinking and feeling. I often used that line during my thirty years as a football coach.

Over the next few years, Johnny taught me many more things about football, sports, winning, losing, and life in general. He taught me trivial information, as well. Some of which got us in trouble. He showed me how we could ride our bikes through the parade that the Powers girls were having. He showed me shortcuts to Parnell's Grocery and how to never pay for RC Colas. Johnny had discovered a spot on the cap of RC colas used to indicate which bottle caps contained the red RC stamp under the cork seal. Bottle caps with RC print were redeemable for a free RC Cola. We collected bottle caps, and would go through them to save the RC caps. Every time we traded a cap for a new bottle of pop, Johnny used his trained eye to select a new winner. He was so good at it that we always had redeemable bottle caps on hand.

Johnny also showed me where we might just strike it rich! Everybody knew that the (Paul) Sansburys vacationed in the mountains most summers. One of their favorite things to do was to hunt for gems, such as rubies, sapphires, and diamonds. They often brought back sacks of dirt containing gems. After they finished sifting through them, they deposited what was remaining in the stream. (The stream runs from the Kilgo pond through the middle of Greenway Drive, all the way to Swift Creek.) Johnny found the deposit of looked-over gem ore, and we decided that there had to be valuable rock material in those samples. We had seen on TV how the old gold miners used pie plates to sift through and find gold and other valuable gems. So we borrowed a couple of Mom's metal pie pans and headed back to our mound of rock materials and started sifting. Once we dipped those pie pans with sand and dirt into the water, and the silt washed away, those remaining rocks shined like gold and diamonds in the sun! We looked at each other in amazement. We had discovered the mother lode! Johnny said we had to keep this secret to ourselves. So we took all the shiny rock material and put it in our pockets, then covered up our small mining operation with tree limbs and pine straw!

We decided it would be best for Johnny to keep the treasures in his room in a small box that he had. After all, he was three grades ahead of me and much more responsible! We also decided that we needed one of those cloth bags that had a drawstring to keep our treasures. Johnny remembered that Mr. Parnell had a bubblegum treat in his candy case called "Gold Nuggets." The bubblegum was packaged inside a small white pouch with drawstrings. So we picked up enough drink bottles to buy two packs of Gold Nuggets and pay the 2 percent sales tax. Then we went to Mr. Parnell's store, traded in the bottles, and bought the gum. We really wanted the pouches more than the gum, but we did manage to chew up all the gum before getting back to our stash at Johnny's house. On the way, we talked about how rich we were going to be. Then reality hit us, and we realized that we had a major problem. Who would we sell our treasures to? A friend of mine at school, Pat, had a father who ran a jewelry store. Where better to sell jewels than to the local jewelry store? Problem solved! Johnny suggested that on Saturday when we went to the movies, we could go early and stop by to talk to Mr. Wells; after all, it was just around the corner from the movie house!

So for the next few days, we sifted more dirt, found more gems, filled our gem sacks, and contemplated being rich. When Saturday arrived, we met and decided not to take our jewels in just yet, but we would still talk to Mr. Wells to see what we should do. I was really nervous when we entered the jewelry store. Mr. Wells was in the back, and he came out when the bell rang as we walked in the door. "Hey boys. How can I help you today?" Johnny spoke up. "Mr. Wells, we were wondering how much you might pay for a sack of jewels." Mr. Wells rubbed his chin and said, "I don't know. It would depend on the kind of jewels, their sizes. and how well cut they are." "Cut?" we both said at the same time. "Yes, jewels are cut to bring out the shine and beauty. Also to fit into rings, necklaces, etc.," replied Mr. Wells. We left the store a little dejected. I asked Johnny what we were going to do. His response was, "Cut them."

We could hardly watch the movies. All we could think of was cutting the stones and getting them sold. We rushed home after leaving the theater and went straight to my dad's shop. We tried everything to cut those dang stones: hacksaws, hatchets, knives. You name it, we tried it. Every once in a while, a stone would chip or crack, and it did produce a shine where it broke, but we never figured out how to cut gemstones.

On Monday after school, we walked back uptown to see Mr. Wells. This time, we showed him our stones. He used that eye thing that jewelers use to study stones and work on jewelry. As he looked and looked, Johnny and I were waiting on him to make us an offer for our sack of stones. As he took off the eye thing and looked up at us, I could see on his face that we were not about to be rich. Then I heard a word I had never heard before—quartz! All of our gems were quartz which apparently is the most common stone in the world and worth nothing to a jeweler. Of course, this was not what we wanted to hear and was very disappointing to us both. We left and stopped in at Parnell's Grocery on the way home and traded in a couple of RC bottle caps for two twelve-ounce RC Colas. By the time we got home, we were pretty much over the disappointment of not striking it rich!

As I reflect back on those few years on Greenway Drive that Johnny Truluck took me under his wing, I realize that he made me feel like I was important and worthy to be his friend. And I realize how much he influenced my life. And when I think of all the fun things we did together and think about the time we "struck it rich," I realize that, indeed, we did strike it rich! A true friend is a lot more valuable than rubies and diamonds. Johnny Truluck was a true friend. I loved Johnny as a friend and still miss him.

Johnny is gone now and has been for a while, but I know he lives on in the hearts and minds of those of us who knew him. He especially lives on in those of who grew up with him on Greenway Drive!

Outfoxing the Foxhole

For the first three years that we lived on Greenway Drive, we stayed in Dr. Wilson's old rental house located near the end of the street. I was but four years old, but I can remember the outside of that house better than the inside. We had a huge front yard—it was the size of a football field. The backyard was small because there was a pond, literally, right behind the house. The only thing that kept me from getting to the pond was a six-foot wire fence that surrounded the pond. There were a couple of big oak trees behind the house, across the fence, that kept the backyard shaded. It was a great place to play, especially during hot summer days. My neighbor and friend Jim Dewitt and I played together a lot in the backyard. We were about the same age and got along good. One day, we talked about building a foxhole, like the ones Army men used. We decided that the back-yard would be a great place to build it. We decided that it had to be big enough for at least three or four Army guys and deep enough so that we could stand up in it and not have our heads sticking out the top. No one wants to get their head shot off.

So we each borrowed our dad's shovels and started digging. It was pretty hard at first because the ground was hard, but once we got past the hard part, it became less dense and more sand and was easier to dig. Before you knew it, we had dug a great ole big hole in my backyard. We played Army all day long in that hole. We played till it was getting close to dark. The next day, we started playing again. Then we decided that it might be cool to cover the top of the hole, and then we could have a fort. So we scrounged around and found scrap wood and limbs and boards, almost anything we could think of; and we covered the top, leaving just a small opening in one end, to crawl into and out of our new fort. Covering the top created some major changes. First, we needed flashlights inside because it was dark. And it was cooler inside the fort than outside. I guess we discovered geothermal energy and didn't know it. And when a rain shower came, all the rain water settled into our fort/foxhole.

Later, Dad got home. He must have heard us playing in the back, and he walked around there and saw what we had built. He was less than excited about our project. He told us we had to fill the hole back with dirt and clean up the mess. And he said that he wanted the yard to look just like it did before we dug the hole. And he wanted it done before suppertime! Well, that pretty much put an end to the fort and to our foxhole, but now we had to undo what it took us two days to do, and we had to do it before dark. So we got busy shoveling the dirt mounds back into the hole. That is when we discovered the most astonishing thing about a hole. If you put back all the dirt that you took out of a hole, it will not fill the hole back up. Not even close. We raked up and shoveled in all the dirt we could find in the yard, and still there wasn't enough. What are we going to do? There was no more dirt anywhere. So we decided to try something else, but we had to get the dirt back out, so we dug the dirt back out of the hole. Then we raked up some leaves and pine straw. We gathered up bricks and twigs and put them in first. Then we covered that with leaves and straw. Then we put the dirt on top of all the rest and smoothed it over. It worked! We passed Dad's inspection. Now whenever I ride down Greenway Drive, I ride down to where the house was that we rented, and I wonder…is there or has there ever been a giant sinkhole where our foxhole used to be?

Dane Smyre Jr.

Looking Back

L ooking back on my formative years growing up in a small town like Darlington conjures up many pleasant memories. As I began jotting them down, they came slowly at first; but then, like a flood, they rushed in, not unlike the rain after a summer monsoon storm pours through a dry Tucson, riverbed in Arizona. It is overwhelming!

We were a creative mix of kids who spent most days somewhere in and around Greenway Drive. There were probably around twenty of us in the immediate vicinity, so at any given time, there were enough of us to get some kind of activity going. With no cell phones, no iPads, and no game consoles, we were forced to use our imagination. And use it we did!

At our disposal were at least five ponds, so fishing came naturally. There were three ponds behind the Dewitts' house. There was the Suggs' Pond and also the pond at Bob Kilgo's place. The Kilgo pond was officially off-limits for us kids, but it was by far the best fishing hole. It was worth the risk to sneak under the fence if we had the chance to hook one of those big bass! Suggs' Pond was probably the largest, and to get to the big fish, one needed a boat. Of course, we had no boat, so we built a raft from inner tubes and plywood. I don't recall that effort yielding many fish, but it sure was fun poling across that pond!

When normal fishing got boring, there were other approaches to pass the time on those hot summer days. One alternative was minifishing with miniature poles and miniature hooks designed to catch minifish, or minnows, in the creek that ran from the Kilgos' Pond down to Swift Creek. Can you imagine?

I mentioned building the raft, but we certainly were not limited to that one endeavor. We were adept at building almost anything! Construction was in our blood. From tree houses to forts and fox-holes, if we built it, all the kids would come for hours and hours of great fun and amusement!

When not in trees, under the ground, or in the water, we were probably exploring in the woods or playing neighborhood games. I remember those treasures found in Army C-ration boxes left behind by weekend warriors during their summer exercises. We unearthed seashells when one of the nearby farmers dug an irrigation ditch. Who knew that Darlington was once the "Myrtle Beach" of its day! Of course, we played sports too! Naturally, there was racing of every kind. We even had our own parade to coincide with the Southern 500 parade. Beauty queens and all! There was football in anyone's yard that was big enough and had no sandspurs. Baseball was played in the closest mowed field. We skateboarded down the Spring Street hill before skateboards were even made. We'd disassemble regular roller skates and attach them to a board, and off we'd go! Once in a while, it would get cold enough in the winter to freeze the shallow pools of water in Williamson Park. Instant hockey rink! One just needed to avoid the cypress knees.

When a break was needed from our grueling schedules, we'd head for "the little store," just a short bike ride away that had all the drinks, candy, and fireworks a kid could wish for. In the summer, wild plums took the place of that candy. They were everywhere. I get a stomachache just thinking about them! When it got too hot, there was swimming at Black Creek, Lake Darpo, and even Bellyache Branch.

What fun…rehashing memories from fifty years ago! Seems like just yesterday! Life truly passes in the blink of the eye. I'm fortunate and extremely blessed to have had the opportunity to "grow" in such a rich environment. Wouldn't trade it for a thing!

Harvey Drawdy

Friends Part 2

Paul and Mary Anne Sansbury

After three years in Dr. Wilson's house at the end of Greenway Drive, Merle and I had an opportunity to buy a small house located at 112 Greenway Drive. Across the street to the right is where Paul and Mary Anne Sansbury lived with their four children: Clevie, Andy, Danny, and Susie. Paul was an attorney, and he held an important government office, as I recall. One morning, Harmon and I were having breakfast at the local hangout, Deluxe Café. The café was owned by Oscar Ballard and had become the local gathering place for coffee and breakfast for many of the Darlington people...especially the older men. This is where men started their day with a good discussion about the town, the state, and even the federal government. Most of the talk centered around tasteless jokes, gossip, or some form of religion or politics. This particular morning, the discussion was focused on a new federal program that would give food stamps to poor families to help them with buying groceries. Several local farmers started their day with an early breakfast at Oscar's café, and they were engaged in a major discussion about the new federal program. One particular farmer was on a rant about this being an end to farmers being able to get farmworkers at an affordable price. I noticed Paul Sansbury, right in the middle of the discussion, baiting the conversation and creating an angry group of farmers. One of the farmers had gotten so angry he was almost foaming at the mouth. It just so happened that Paul had brought the local newspaper with him, as he did most mornings. That particular day, the paper had done a feature article about the federal government's new giveaway program. The first part of the article included the new food stamp assistance program and how it worked. The second part of the article was about the new land bank program that essentially provided incentive money to farmers who would place a portion of their tillable land into the land bank and not plant certain crops or raise certain livestock. In addition, the paper listed all the Darlington County farmers who had opted into the new program. Apparently, they were being paid $30 an acre not to plant. That could mean thousands of dollars in government money going to the biggest farms. As Paul started reading aloud the names and the number of acres each farmer had put into the land bank, you would have thought the café was on fire. The farmers vanished from the restaurant. I remember Paul as a fair and honest man. He was a God-fearing man and led by example. His wife, Mary Anne, was great with all the kids in the neighborhood.

Jim Brown Sr.

After we moved up the street to 112 Greenway Drive, I had the privilege of meeting and making friends with my next-door neighbor, Jim Brown. Jim was a contractor and built homes for a living. He was a very kind and considerate man. Jim was a part owner of a beach house in Cherry Grove. South Carolina. He, along with Bob and John Kilgo, shared ownership of the raised beach house, just a block from the ocean. They took apart a local house and then rebuilt it on a beach lot. I went with them one weekend to paint the house. It was me, Robert Mills, John, and Bob Kilgo. We went down on a Friday after work, started painting early Saturday, and had the whole house painted by 2:00 p.m. Then we went to an all-you-could-eat oyster roast for $5 and ate every oyster the man had in the coolers. They had to shut the restaurant doors because we had eaten them out of business. I used to tell people that it took five gallons of paint and three fifths of whiskey to get that beach house painted. Maybe that had something to do with our appetites that day.

STAN DRAWDY AND KEITH CARTER

Jim was very generous with the beach house. He allowed me and my family to use it on many occasions. He was also generous with his pickup truck camper. It was self-contained and slept up to six people. I had a pickup truck, and he let us use that camper on one of our vacations to the mountains. My boys rode in the back, and we traveled all over the mountains of North Carolina and Tennessee for over a week. Having use of the camper allowed us to go from place to place in the mountains without a lot of work. It was a great vacation that we still talk about today. Thanks, Jim!

Bill Cain Sr.

Bill Cain and I became friends because we both were principals in the same school district, and we attended several professional conferences and scores of meetings together over the years. One of the most memorable conferences was held in Dallas, Texas. Bill drove his car, and I rode with him. If you really want to get to know someone, ride halfway across the country with them and then back again. Bill Cain was a man of culture and refinement…unlike many of us who were educated beyond our intelligence. Bill actually had a BA degree in Latin. In his early days as an educator, he coached boys' basketball and also tennis. He served as tennis coach as well as principal up until the day he retired.

On our trip to Dallas, we went through Tyler, Texas…the Rose Capital of the World. Bill insisted that we take the time to enjoy several of the rose gardens that catered to the public. We finally got to Dallas and to the convention center and got registered. I attended the elementary-level conference while Bill sat in on the high school meetings. I think we both probably learned more than we would admit, and we did see a part of the country while traveling and while in Texas. It was a great trip.

I do remember that we were operating on a shoestring budget, so we skipped breakfast and ate sandwiches for lunch so that we would have enough to splurge at the end of the week and dine out at the Cattlemen's Club. It was world-famous and featured in the TV series *Dallas*. I kept my eyes out, just in case J. R. Ewing happened to come into the restaurant, but he didn't. With all our penny-pinching all week, we just did have enough for a T-bone steak and baked potato. They did serve us a dish of mountain oysters as an appetizer. I hate to admit it, but they were quite tasty. Bill and I both cleaned the plate. That was quite an experience, and getting to know Bill Cain the way I did was icing on the cake.

Here are some of my fondest memories of Bill. He had a green thumb. Always planted a small garden, and he had the best vineyard in Darlington. And he shared his grapes with the neighborhood. His speaking accent was very unique. His Low Country brogue was very similar to a Boston-type accent. His speech grabbed your attention and kinda mesmerized his listeners. He served as both principal and coach for many years. Not many people would have the time or stamina to accomplish those at the same time. He always looked out for the underprivileged kids in his school. No one knows the number of prom dresses, tuxedos, school lunches, tennis shoes, and the like that he discreetly provided his students over the years. Bill came from a family in the Moncks Corner area who lost their huge farm and plantation when a power company created Lake Moultrie and Lake Marion and started a public electric co-op. His homeplace still exists under one of those big lakes. I also found it interesting that Bill Cain, with help from a few high school boys, built the house on Greenway Drive that he and Mrs. Cain lived in and raised their family.

Keith Carter

Mosquito Truck

The mosquito truck would come around fogging our neighborhood with a spray that was supposed to keep down the mosquito population. It's possible the pesticide used was DDT, but I remember it having a kerosene smell, so it could have been that or some kind of mixture. I don't remember how often the truck would come up and down our street, but it seems that it was at least every two weeks during the warm part of the year. The fogger was aimed to the right side of the truck as it drove down the street, so by making a pass both ways, the driver covered both sides of each street as he made his way around town.

I had a pair of swim goggles that I would put on when I heard the truck coming, and then I would run out to the edge of our yard and stand there while the mosquito truck came by, shooting its mysterious fog toward our house. I would hold my breath during the direct pass, but I couldn't hold it long, and I'm sure I breathed in plenty of it as it rolled across our yard, seeking mosquito eggs and larvae to kill. I wore the goggles just because I had them, and I thought it made a cool statement to be able to keep my eyes open during the fogging. I had seen pictures of soldiers wearing gas masks with goggles during warfare, and that had impressed me, and this was the best I could do to play my part.

I am a little surprised that my mother did not intervene and prevent me from doing what seems now like a crazy and reckless thing, but I can only say that I never asked her permission and never thought to tell her about it, so she possibly never knew. Or maybe she thought it was normal, being the free spirit that she was. If any neighbors saw me standing like a statue as the truck rolled by, they were never moved to tell my parents and probably thought that whatever I might get served me right. I know the mosquito truck driver had to see me, but I doubt that I was the only dunce who did it, and he sure didn't seem to care; it was a free country.

What I can tell you is that I never had any problems from it, and furthermore, over the course of my life, I have never been bothered by mosquitos. Tonda, Esme, Libby, and I could be sitting on our patio many years later; and they were pure mosquito bait, while I was the opposite. They would be slapping and scratching, wanting to go in, and I'd be saying, "What's the matter?" And if a mosquito did stray over and bite me, it didn't affect me as it did them. So my outrageous acts of self-fumigation may seem foolhardy and crazy in our present world of safety to the max, but I must say that I'm pretty happy with the way things turned out!

I Know Why the Caged Parakeet Sings

When we lived on Greenway Drive, our mother bought us a parakeet from Rose's dime store on the square. He (or she) was green, and we named him (or her) Petey.

Petey lived in a typical parakeet cage which we kept near a window in our added-on dining room. The eat-in kitchen in our house had become too small for a family of five, so just after my sister Shelley was born, my father contracted with George Miller to add on to the front of the house. We gained a dining room and a nice screened-in front porch. It was just after the expansion that we got Petey, now that we had enough room for a birdcage. Like all parakeets, all Petey did was hop around on his little wooden perch, stepping sideways to the left and then to the right, chirping all the time and acting nervous. The cage was equipped with a little feeding trough and a water bowl, both of which hung from the wire walls. There was also a white slab of stone attached to the wire cage which he could rub his beak on, to sharpen it, I guess, or maybe to file it down. I doubt that Petey really knew what he was doing, but what he did, he did faithfully.

We would buy him treats which were made of seeds molded into the shape of a bell, which we hung from the top of the cage. He pecked on the seed bell as an alternative to eating from his feeding trough. He also had a real little bell and a mirror. The mirror was to make him think he wasn't alone, and he could peck at the bell to make some extra noise. We kept a layer of newspaper in the bottom of the cage to catch his droppings and all the seed hulls and feathers that fell, which all together was a lot.

We tried to teach him to talk, and sometimes we thought he actually repeated some words back to us, but we couldn't be sure it wasn't accidental. Mostly, he just did his little whistling chirps. He would look at us intently with one of his eyes, turning his head ninety degrees since each of his eyes was where our temples are. It must have been confusing to have seen totally different scenes with each eye, but that's the way many birds and other animals (like rabbits) are made. I wondered if he could turn off what his other eye was seeing while he was looking at us with this one. I'll never know.

Sometimes, my mother would feel sorry for Petey, caged up all the time as he was, and would take his cage out to the screen porch and open the cage door so he could get out; but he was so accustomed to being in the cage that the open door didn't register in his dense, little bird brain. I remember it taking him quite a while, if not forever, to discover that he could escape from his cage into the porch, which was really just a much larger cage. We would get impatient and reach in with our finger extended for him to step onto and then bring him out of the cage. We would do things like let him sit on our shoulder, and before long, he was trying out his wings around the porch. It did us good to see him stretch his wings and fly around, which he could never do in the cage. We thought he enjoyed it, and maybe he did, but I know now that it was vicarious thinking that we were doing.

Mother always warned us about going in and out of the screen door while Petey was loose on the porch. But one day the inevitable happened—the screen door was opened, and Petey flew out. He flew away from the house, and we were able to follow him until he lit in a tree in a neighbor's yard a couple of houses down. He was just a green speck, but we kept our eyes on him. We knew it was hopeless to chase him. But soon he flew farther away, and we lost sight of him. We definitely thought he was gone forever. But we took it well, never being real pet fanatics. He was just a dime store parakeet, and we could always get another one—maybe a blue one next time.

We soon forgot about it as we played around the house with the neighbor kids that day. But after a couple of hours, I heard a familiar chirping from the large walnut tree across the street. Recognizing his sound, we began looking for him in the tree until we found him sitting there, nervous as usual, hopping left and right on a limb. He was watching us, chirping all the time, and he hopped to lower branches in the tree as he watched us watch him. I ran to tell Mother that Petey was back, and he was across the street! She came out and said, "I think he wants to come back home." She went inside and got his cage and a stool, which she placed in the middle of the front yard with the door open. Then she herded all of us kids into the screen porch to watch.

Petey continued to descend in the walnut tree, little by little, and finally he got to the lowest branch. He stayed there for what seemed like a very long time to us, but it probably wasn't even a minute, and then he flew across the street and lit on a limb of the little dogwood tree that our father had set out in the yard. He was close to the cage now; and he could see his food and water inside, his mirror and his bell, his white rock, his wooden perch, his newspaper carpeting—all so familiar and inviting! He had been free for a while and probably had not found a single seed out there or a drop of water. I'm sure he was famished and worn-out from the flying which he wasn't used to. He flew to the birdcage and lit on top of it. Then he walked

STAN DRAWDY AND KEITH CARTER

across the top and skittered down to the open door, where he stood on the threshold for a while, and then hopped inside onto his perch.

Mother went out promptly and shut and latched the door and brought the cage back inside. Petey ate and drank, ate and drank, and he sang like never before! He was really a happy bird! He had found his freedom and had probably thought at first that it was great. But he soon realized that while he had freedom, he also had no food or water, and he had no idea how to find it. Luckily for him, he didn't learn about predators, but being a bright-green bird would have made him an easy target for an owl or a hawk or a cat. And maybe he missed us—our voices, our play, our laughter. It was all he had ever known.

Maya Angelou wrote a book about her life entitled *I Know Why the Caged Bird Sings*. She had left home at an early age and lived a life of freedom; but her existence was filled with want, need, and danger, and was devoid of any joy. She learned of the contrast of freedom versus security, and of the happiness that came from being a willing and safe "captive" at home with her family. Petey could have written a book by that title if birds could write books; his brief experience had certainly given him the credentials. And it seemed to us that his singing was happier than ever!

Cyndie Wall Geries

Greenway Drive Part 2

While my dad was assigned to Japan, we lived across the street from the Sansbury family from 1954 until 1955. Who could possibly forget all of the exciting times shared and the kindness extended by this family? Mother did not drive, so Paul drove me to school regularly. Every school morning, I walked over to watch Captain Kangaroo with Clevie and Andy. None of them were old enough to attend school at this time. Danny and Susie were yet to be born. Paul would transport me to school in his big black Chevrolet. Mary Anne created a fabulous yard designed for extensive play—a sandbox, seesaw, monkey bars, swings—and a shared front yard for more games of kickball, red rover, chase, and hide-and-go-seek than one could count. After Dad's death at age thirty-two, Mom purchased our home on Evans Circle. Mary Anne quickly filled two bushel baskets with cement to provide a step on either side of the short fence that divided our yards. Those cement steps provided access from our yard to theirs. Some may remember the grape arbor in that same area where our yards adjoined. We learned of four-o'clocks, stokesia, camellias, and many other species in those back-yard flower beds. There was also a persimmon tree near the monkey bars. Right below the grapevine, Mary Anne created a set of steps made of collected rocks. The steps led us down the hill to the creek that we loved so much. For years, we tried to catch minnows, turtles, and any number of species in that creek. Lots of Girl Scout activities were hosted around those rock steps and the creek area. When Evans Circle was being prepared for paving, Mary Anne used large pieces of unearthed petrified wood from the dirt road to develop a little garden area near the creek. She poured cement and had the children put their footprints in the cement at the base of large pieces of petrified wood. I also remember that the Sansbury family had a rock-polishing machine on their screened porch. I remember feeding Danny and Susie baby food on the porch, as well as enjoying Kool-Aid and popcorn there regularly in the afternoons. We played in their garage. Kids able to tell time on the hour were allowed to advance one step up on their wooden ladder.

Mary Anne taught us to swim in Black Creek at the Darlington Country Club access area. Mom did not swim but was thankful for Mary Ann's commitment to offer swimming lessons via the Red Cross for many years. I will never forget summer trips to Lawton Park in Hartsville. How about those huge all-day suckers? Again, thanks to Mary Anne for many lessons in nature, play, and love. Once when I was babysitting the kids, Danny stuck a piece of corn from the bird feeder up his nose. I think Dr. Wilson had to extract the corn when it began to swell in his nasal passage. Mary Ann even knitted a Christmas stocking for me early on, as well as a ski sweater upon high school graduation.

The Welch Family: When not teaching biology, coaching football, or hunting, Jimmy spent a great deal of time downstairs watching TV. Belva was a great cook and mother to Butch and Barbara. Barbara and I spent the majority of one hot summer playing dolls at their house. I wonder how many trips we made up and down the steps in their split-level home. By the way, I often saw Barbara heading to feed the bird dogs many afternoons. Butch often cut our grass. I remember when we took lifesaving swimming lessons at the Darlington Country Club when their pool was brand-new. Mary Anne Sansbury was the instructor.

Mother, Fran, and I rented a house while my dad, a US Marine, was serving an eight-month tour of duty in Japan. Nancy, Jimmy, Robbie, and Jimbo Brown lived to the left. I attended first grade at Brunson-Dargan Elementary and have fond memories of my teacher who told us she had eyes in the back of her head. I truly believed her. One highlight of my first-grade school year was the Halloween carnival when Noni Bonnoitt was the fortune-teller. Other parents supervised assorted games, contests, and food booths. All the children wore costumes and enjoyed the festivities. May Day was another first-grade special school event. Each student dressed for the occasion. The girls wore dresses and homemade hats. The boys were decked out wearing bow ties. We celebrated at the ball field.

When I was in the fourth grade, sitting on our screened porch on Evans Street while making an endless number of potholders to sell was a hot venture during the summer. The money earned would serve to finance our next neighborhood project. Among the projects, I remember charging ten cents per doll carriage ride down the hill in our backyard and across the creek. We created a mini putt-putt golf game too. Speaking of the creek, I wonder how many turtles, salamanders, and frogs we caught. As a result of exploring woods, the creek, and the park, I was constantly covered in poison oak/ivy. I also remember gathering straw and digging tunnels on the vacant lot across the street from our house. This lot was eventually purchased by Mae and Cleve Scott. They built a brick ranch-style house. We were so excited the night Helen Scott got married at their home. I also recall that Sandra Scott and Robbie Brown played high school tennis. Judy Scott was born when Clyde, Helen, and Sandra were older. I can still see Judy standing in the playpen in their den. I will never forget the throw that Mae crocheted and gifted to me when I was grown. Her divinity candy was the best ever and always a welcomed Christmas gift to our family. Mae and Mother enjoyed a lifelong friendship after all the children were grown and gone.

Playing with dolls was a favorite pastime. Robbie Brown had a Terrie Lee doll that I adored. I can still see her playing the record player to the tune of "Come Along and Be My Party Doll." Jimbo was a loyal comic book collector and artist. He ate lots of raw hotdogs from the icebox on their screened porch.

For a period of time, I kept Brent Sansbury from after school until Dot or Howard got home from work. Brent, Wayne, and Ken Howle were busy boys playing outside most afternoons. Ken Howle regularly reminded us that he was Mike Nelson, Underwater Sea Hunt Man. Bicycle races were frequently observed. After all, time trials were part of the necessary preparation for the neighborhood Southern 500 race day. Girls spent hours decorating wagons, mini-floats, and baby strollers, and serving Kool-Aid and snacks. Jeff and Pete Sansbury usually joined in on the time trails too.

Sarah Cain always had fun birthday parties. I remember well the time Billy tried to break into their new bathroom when the "all girls" birthday party guests were trying out their new bathtub. I spent many hours on the Cains' porch waiting for Sarah to finish her piano practice sessions. I can almost taste that delicious fried chicken that L' Ester regularly prepared. For sure, she was an accomplished cook! Once in a while, we would sneak some scraps to the cats and kittens. Mr. Cain kept us on our toes with garden projects, gathering pine straw and assisting with the "leather" that he made from dried apricots. My favorite part was rolling the sheets in granulated sugar. That process was a labor of love.

Growing up on Greenway Drive was a fabulous lifestyle, unbeknownst to most of us at the time. Speaking of the "time," most of the neighborhood children were born in the mid- to late '40s, the 1950s, or the early 1960s. What a privilege it was to live in such carefree times. We were a strong, creative, resilient, and a fairly naïve group of kids. We operated as a large family for the most part. Older kids taught younger ones how to ride bikes, skate, play team sports, and become junior entrepreneurs. Most of the houses were fairly modest, with nature abounding. There were empty fields, pine thickets, creeks, ponds, and paved and unpaved roads. I often wonder how many forts, tree houses, and hideouts we created. Green pine cone fights, digging tunnels, making straw houses, fishing, and lots of competitive games were the norm. We did not look for roadblocks and charged on with individual and group activities. Nothing much scared us. The older kids helped raise the younger ones, and fights were rare.

The biggest neighborhood theme events revolved around multiple activities based on the Southern 500 races. Ingram Truluck and Leonard Ballard were in charge and organized model car, bicycle, roller-skating, stroller, and wagon races. Along with the Southern 500 theme came fundraisers to purchase necessary parade decor, beauty queen activities, and award prizes. Ingram served as the announcer and pretty much led the organizational aspects of many race-related activities. I might add that few activities interfered with his snake catching/collection hobby. What about that boa constrictor that got away? I know those snake cages were fairly near the creek where Barbara Truluck, Evalyn Kilgo, and I constantly played. We fished with safety pin hooks; gathered mussels; and caught turtles and lots of tadpoles and frogs. Barbara reminded me a couple of years ago that we cooked grits on candles and built a fire to cook fish. We got tired of cleaning the fish and started frying them whole. She said that Andy Sansbury was our best customer and even went back home to get more money to buy some more fried fish!

From left to right: Andy Sansbury, Bimmy Bonnoitt, Clevie Sansbury, and Punk Bonnoitt.

The Sansburys' and Kilgos' front yards served to host all manner of sports-related competitions. Kickball, football, tag, red rover, Mother May I, hopscotch, tumbling and gymnastics, and putt-putt golf were but a few of the activities we enjoyed. I can see Jimmy Bonnoitt cutting cartwheels and flips regularly. I might add that most of us thought the swimming pool in the Bonnoitts' backyard was of Olympic size. Reflecting now, it was probably only eight by ten feet. Their playhouse was probably smaller than the pool but enormous in my eyes. While on the subject of the Bonnoitts, I can see Sandra instructing her siblings around their dining room table daily after school. She would direct and correct all of their homework! I'm surprised that she became a nurse rather than a teacher. By the way, I must recognize Sandra for her love of ice scraped from the freezer on their back porch. Did she once get her tongue stuck to the freezer? I did covet the transistor radio that Linda Bonnoitt owned when we were in junior high. Linda had the ability to digest more sour weeds than most. Punk had skills like Johnny and Pop Bonnoitt had. There was little of a mechanical nature that he could not solve. How many remember Pop loading us up on his flatbed truck and taking us to his farm off the Lamar Highway to drink unpasteurized milk? I think all of the animals the Bonnoitts had on Greenway Drive, which were generous gifts from their granddaddy. Much to my mother's dismay, one of their goats ate a weeping willow in our backyard…oops! I don't know why we did not charge to view the zoo animals the Bonnoitts collected. That peacock could have funded more neighborhood projects!

In 2017, Greenway Drive neighbors and former residents enjoyed their second reunion, in the Sansburys' backyard. It was a fabulous opportunity to visit and share. Many thanks to those who encouraged us to document personal memories!

Stan Drawdy

The Ice Capades

According to Google and Wikipedia, the Ice Capades were traveling entertainment shows featuring theatrical ice-skating performances by retired Olympic skaters. These shows prospered from the 1940s until the 1990s. Sometimes, these shows would air on one of our two TV channels, in Florence and in Columbia. One was CBS, and the other was NBC. The point is that most of us kids on Greenway Drive had seen ice-skating, but it wasn't something that Southern kids knew much about. We had no ice rinks or ski slopes nearby, so those types of activities were considered foreign to us, except on those rare occasions when it would snow, or we would have an ice storm.

Granted, snow and ice were pretty rare on Greenway Drive in the 1950s and 1960s but not nearly as rare as it is today. I've heard many say that "global warming" and "climate change" are responsible for the weather. Others say that weather occurs in cycles, always has, and always will. All I know is when we were kids, "Mother Nature" controlled the weather; and apparently, she worked for God, Who was ultimately in control of everything. That is why in the winter, kids would pray for snow and ice because those were the only two events that closed schools. Today, when schools are closed due to hurricanes, no one has prayed for those. Viruses can shut down schools, and even businesses. I've even seen heavy rains shut schools down around here.

Anyway, back to snow and ice. Those were the most special times. That's when we got to use our heavy coats, toboggans and gloves, and rubber boots! Or you could put plastic bags over your

145

shoes and use rubber bands around them to hold them on. An inch of snow was like manna from heaven to us kids. We would play all day long out in the cold, only going inside to warm up a bit around the old oil furnace.

A cup of hot chocolate or a bowl of Mom's snow cream—those were the days. Every kid in the neighborhood would be outside playing or on Spring hill with cardboard boxes and plastic bins sliding down the hill all the way to Swift Creek bridge at Williamson Park. If the temperature was really cold, the snow would freeze overnight and could sometimes last for several days. And occasionally it would get cold enough that the ponds would freeze over. We could throw rocks and sticks and boards onto the pond, and they would hit and skip way out onto the ice. And sometimes the ice was thick enough that one could walk out on the ice, even though we had been told never to do that by our parents. But living down South, how many chances does a guy get to be in the Ice Capades?

In our neighborhood, there were two, no, three ponds, thus three skating rinks available whenever ponds froze over: Dr. Wilson's Pond, Kilgos' Pond, and Suggs' Pond. Many of the kids were aware of the near-fatal event when Pete Sansbury had tried to walk or skate (in shoes) across Kilgos' Pond, and the ice broke through, and Pete almost drowned. If not for the friend he was with that day, he would probably not have made it.

So we all were aware of the risks and dangers, and we had been told by our parents many times that if we got out on that ice and it broke and we drowned, then we would get a beating of a lifetime! Nonetheless, during one particular snowstorm, Johnny and I were playing, and we were talking about the ponds being frozen and the story of how Pete almost died.

Honestly, I don't remember if I double-dog dared Johnny or if he double-dog dared me; but there was at least one, maybe two double-dog dares thrown out to walk all the way across a frozen pond! Keep in mind that a double-dog dare is the pinnacle of dares. A double-dog dare is to dares what Amazon is to retail sales. You get the point. You would be the biggest wuss of all wusses not to accept that dare.

Now all we needed was to pick the pond to cross. Dr. Wilson's Pond was too close to Johnny's house, and the Suggs' Pond was too open to people passing by. We certainly didn't want to get caught and drown on the same day! So we decided to go to Kilgos' Pond, which was where Pete almost died. Kilgos' Pond was fenced in and back in the woods. At least if we drowned there, we wouldn't be seen or caught doing what we knew not to do!

As we made our way over to Kilgos' Pond, I was a bit nervous, actually scared to death. As we crawled under the fence in the spot near the spillway where rainwater had washed away some dirt, leaving a gap under the fence just big enough for a kid to crawl through, I remember thinking, *Why am I doing this?* Then I remembered… double-dog dare. As we stood on the bank, Johnny said, "Let me get halfway before you start." I watched Johnny as he slowly inched his way out onto the ice. The sounds of the ice creaking and crackling was terrifying, to say the least. As I stepped onto the ice, I was horrified. I expected to fall through at any point. And what would I do if Johnny went down?

At one point, I froze because it felt like the ice was breaking under my feet. I looked up, and Johnny was climbing onto the other side of the pond. He said, "Come on. You can make it!" With his encouragement, I slowly inched my way across. As I reached the dry land, he grabbed my hand and said, "We made it!"

I've heard it said that God protects drunks and fools. We were not drunk, but we were very foolish. Thank you, Lord!

Gregg Suggs

The Story of the Double Taxi

The year would have been around 1967, as I remember being in the eighth grade at Brunson-Dargan Junior High. The whole story starts with my parents (Willie and Vivian) being out of town at an insurance convention, leaving me and my older brother Glenn at home for the weekend. Glenn had invited our cousins from Greensboro down to stay with us that weekend, and they were a bit more mischievous than Glenn and myself (I'm sure everyone remembers how shy and well-mannered we were).

So here's the story: Around 12:30 a.m., my cousins came up with the idea of calling a taxi to someone's house (close enough so we can enjoy the show) and asking that the driver just pull in the driveway, blow the horn twice, come up to the front door, and get some luggage. Glenn and I agreed that the Powers family was the perfect target for this little adventure, and I remember that the youngest of the Powers girls was a baby at that time. Keep in mind the Powers lived on Greenway Drive and we lived on Spring Street but could see their house. We could hardly contain ourselves as we saw the taxi crossing the bridge at the park on Spring Street heading for the Powers house. Just as instructed, the driver pulled in the driveway, honked the horn two times, and got out of his car heading for the front door. We're all crouched in the little ditch in front of our house on Spring Street, watching the show begin. The driver followed instructions perfectly and rang the doorbell, and seconds later, the front porch light popped on, the front door opened, and there was Mrs. Bunny Powers (she didn't seem too happy). She then proceeded to give the driver an earful about being at her house at this time of the morning and she also had a small baby in the house and no one in her household had called a taxi.

Well, we're rolling around laughing and just so pleased with how all this had played out. The poor taxi driver apologized and backed down the steps to his car and turned out of their driveway headed toward Evans Street to circle back around to Spring Street. Mrs. Bunny closed the door and turned out the porch light, and we imagined back to bed for some sleep. Now, if you remember, the title of this article is "The Story of the Double Taxi," so, yeah, you guessed it. My crazy cousins had called another taxi company in town and told them to head to the Powers house about five minutes after calling the first one. The timing could not have been more perfect, because as the first taxi was pulling off Evans Street, what did we see but the second cab crossing the bridge on Spring Street? You can imagine our delight of anticipating how this was going to play out with Mrs. Bunny just getting settled back in. Well, the second driver followed instructions perfectly also (pull up, blow the horn twice, and come up to the front porch for some luggage), except he didn't get all the way up to the front door. Mrs. Bunny must not have been too settled in as she flung open the front door and started laying into the guy about being at her house this time of morning. The driver apologized, stating he's just doing as instructed by whomever requested the taxi, and left the house. We're now beside ourselves, rolling around laughing so hard and just proud of our masterful prank on our neighbors.

On Monday at school, as I was walking to class, who did I see beaming right toward me but one of the Powers girls? She proceeded to let me know that her parents knew it was us Suggs boys behind the double taxi trick and that my parents would hear about this when they got back from their trip. I, of course, played absolutely dumbfounded by her accusations and did not know what she was referring to. I do remember Willie questioning us about all this, but we put all the blame on the Greensboro cousins, and it just blew over. Over the years, I've had some good laughs with James, Bunny, and the girls about this little story, and confessed to what they knew all along—that Glenn and I were involved.

I will say that the whole Greenway Drive/Spring Street area was an absolute great place to grow up. I developed some great lifelong friendships, not only with the kids whom I grew up with but also with some of their parents as time passed on. I have so many pleasant memories of my childhood and teenage years from the neighborhood and feel truly blessed to have grown up there.

PS: When I told Glenn I was submitting this story, he reminded me that we actually called a third cab that night, but that one never showed up. I don't remember if we really called the third, but I told him I just don't believe we would have stooped that low!

Barbara Truluck Benjamin

Greenway Drive Snake Stories

I t all started when Dot and Charlie Truluck took their children—
Ingram, Barbara, and Johnny—to Florida in 1956. One of the
places we visited was Ross Allen's Snake Farm, and we were amazed
because this man stood in the middle of a big room full of rattlesnakes. Instantly, Ingram fell in love with snakes, and when we
returned home, he got a book on snakes and began studying and
learning as much as he could about them. Not only did our neighborhood have a lot of places to play, but it was also full of great places
to look for snakes. We had streams, woods, ponds, and even Swift
Creek that runs through Williamson Park on Spring Street.

Ingram and Keith Carter started their adventure by watching a
snake in Dr. Wilson's dad's pond. This is one of the three ponds that
were very close to our home. Keith got tired of waiting on the snake,
so he went home, but Ingram stayed and waited patiently, and then
suddenly, Ingram saw his chance to catch the snake, so he dove into
the pond and grabbed the snake. Of course, it bit him! He ran home
with the snake, and Papa (our grandfather) took the snake and killed
it. Our parents put the snake in a shoebox and rushed Ingram to
Dr. Wilson's clinic. Lucas Dargan just happened to be there; and he
looked at the snake and said it was not poisonous, it was just a water
snake. Ingram, still crying, said, "I told you it was not poisonous."
He was only about eight and a half at the time, so my parents were

151

not sure he knew the difference, but turns out, he knew exactly what he was talking about. After this, the snake hunt was on.

Some of the girls and boys in the neighborhood also learned to identify all kinds of snakes. Here is a list of the snakes that I can remember that we caught: hognose, ringnecks, cone noses, blacksnakes, rat snakes, corn snakes, king snakes, coral king snakes, green snakes, mud snakes, rainbow snakes, glass snakes, garter snakes, and of course water snakes. We'd put them in jars, keep them for a while, and then release them. One Sunday, Ingram left the jars on the wrong side of the house, and while we were at church, the sun came out, and it was too hot, and the snakes died. We were devastated. After that, my dad had our neighbor, Bruce Lynch, build us ten cages in our woods. We now had a safe, cool place to keep our snakes until we let them go.

In 1959, Ingram, then about twelve years old, decided to order a six-foot black indigo snake from South America with the approval of our parents. When the snake arrived at the Darlington Train Depot, they called mom and told her to come get the snake immediately, and she did. Mom let Ingram keep this big six-foot snake in his bedroom, in a big wooden box. Of course, the snake would get loose when we were at school. Mom and Martha, the wonderful lady who did our ironing, would get the broom and somehow get the snake back in the box. Eventually, Mom ended up holding this six-foot snake. She really was a good sport about all of this.

Trulucks
Upper: Barbara, Ingram with a five-foot boa constrictor, and Johnny.
Lower: their mother, Dot, with a six-foot indigo snake.

After this snake, Ingram and the other kids decided to get a five-foot boa constrictor, but we had to make money to pay for it. I think the snake cost about $12. So some of us, along with our friends, set up tables with Kool-Aid, crackers, and candy to sell. We did okay but needed more money. So we decided to have a fish fry in our woods. Getting the fish would not be a problem, because my little brother Johnny was great at fishing, and he and some others could catch all the fish we would need from Dr. Wilson's dad's pond and the two Dewitt ponds because they were loaded with fish.

The girls cooked the grits over candles, and the boys fried the fish over a campfire. Business was great, and everyone said it was delicious. The only problem was that business was so good that we couldn't clean the fish fast enough to keep up with the cooking orders, so we stopped cleaning the fish and just cut off the heads and fried them. Our best customer was Andy Sansbury, and he kept going home to get more money and said it was the best fish he had ever eaten. We never told anyone what we had done until we had a neighborhood reunion in 1998. I told his mom, Mary Anne Sansbury, about us cooking the uncleaned fish and about her son Andy eating them and saying they were delicious. She didn't say much and laughed a little. I can't believe we did that, but when you are a little kid, some things just don't seem too bad.

Back to the fundraising. After the fish fry, we had enough money to buy the boa constrictor. Ingram ordered the snake, and again, the Darlington Train Depot called and told Mom to come and get the snake immediately. Now it was time to go to visit our grandparents in Anderson, South Carolina, and Mom said the snake could not go! Well, about halfway on the trip, Ingram pulled out a pillowcase with the snake in it, and poor Mom, she just kept on driving. Incidentally, Ingram named the snake Charlie. My grandparents were okay about the snake coming, I think. My aunt called the Anderson newspaper, and they came and did an article and took pictures. When we got home, we kept the five-foot snake outside in a very big wooden box covered with a screen, a heavy board, and cement blocks on top to keep him from escaping; but one day when we went to get the snake, he was gone. He had pushed the boards and the bricks off. We never saw him again, but we certainly got a lot of phone calls from people. One even said that they had seen a snake stretched from one side of the road to the other side of the road. This type of snake cannot live in cold weather, so he would have died when the winter came.

When Ingram became a teenager, he started catching copperheads (a poisonous snake). Fortunately, he never got bitten by one of those.

Later, someone gave him another boa constrictor. He brought it home and put it in a pillowcase and tied it closed and put it under the house for a night. Well, you know what happened—the snake escaped, and we couldn't find him. One day, our mom smelled something horrible, and she knew that the snake had died under our house. She wasn't about to let a dead snake stay under the house.

So she put on a raincoat, rubber boots, rubber gloves, and a rain hat; and she crawled up under the house and found that snake and dragged him out. Not many people would have done this, but she did. That was the last exotic snake we had.

As you read this story, it is very evident that our parents were great sports, very understanding, and very supportive of their children's adventures. I would like to thank all the kids and parents for making Greenway Drive the most special place to grow up.

Over a hundred people came back for the 1998 Greenway Drive reunion. Everyone brought a picnic lunch; and we all ate, told stories, and listened to Harvey Drawdy sing in our front yard. We all had a great time.

Fran Wall Weaver

Our Neighborhood Part 3

Memories on Medford

While spending the night at Cynthia Smyre's home, Eloise pulled her rocking chair into the middle of the floor close to the den TV, all set up with popcorn, to watch the *Twilight Zone*. This series began in 1959 and ran through 1964. The science fiction program was a horror, fantasy anthology. This night, a teenage girl was asleep, fell off her bed, and went through her bedroom wall ending up in the fifth dimension. Believe me, we kids were in Eloise's lap or around her feet, and I did not sleep a wink that night! Many games were played in the Smyres' large front yard. Across the street was a field of cows. Let me tell you, that big fierce bull stalked me when I wore my red-hooded car coat. Barbara Truluck and Becky Greer enjoyed stretching out in the field beside the Dixie Mechanics Club amongst the cows and between the cow patties. They took little rest periods gazing at the clouds, finding interesting shapes. Thank goodness that big fierce bull wasn't in their fenced-in area! (Years later, I had the privilege of picking up Cynthia at the Miami Airport as she returned from missionary work in Bogota, Colombia—see how friendship spans the years?)

Ingram Truluck and Keith Carter

Beautiful, put-together Dot Truluck amazed me! She was very tolerant of her handsome, kind son Ingram's love of snakes. He kept his collection in his bedroom, even in his chest of drawers, I think, plus in his backyard cages. Many days, he would have one wrapped around his neck and arms. We were placed on alert as notices went out on telephone poles when one of his creepy-crawlies had escaped, especially the expensive BOA CONSTRICTOR. At the 2017 Greenway reunion, Keith Carter confessed he and Ingram had paid an exorbitant amount of money for their new pet. (You may remember the boys set up a store to raise money for their many projects. They bought crackers and separated and repackaged them as a fundraiser!) While those two found great pleasure in snake ownership, I had nightmares (FOR YEARS). I am still trying to forgive Ingram and Keith. I do not know how the dear Carter family felt about Keith's passionate attraction to those scary reptiles. Oh my goodness, I was floored recently when my dear, thoughtful friend Barbara Truluck admitted she had a few snakes in her room also! Sakes alive! No! SNAKES alive!

All of the Bonnoitts

Punk got a wonderful fast-moving go-kart from Santa Claus. On Christmas morning, his dad, Johnny, had him practicing his new ride right near their driveway on Evans Circle. Bimmy and I kept begging to have a turn. Punk insisted we should not, that we would wreck his new Christmas wheels. Bimmy was persistent, and finally thoughtful Johnny gave in. Punk was fretting as Bimmy got situated in the driver's seat. Johnny helped squeeze me in on Bimmy's right side. Next thing I knew, Bimmy had put the pedal to the metal; and Holy Smoke, we did just what nervous Punk feared—we didn't go one inch forward, just made a hard left, driving straight into their side yard fence. We bounced off, and Punk immediately fell to the ground in despair. I can still hear his repetitive shouts of "I Told You So!"

I have to say our friend Punk was a bit prone to accidents. He was wounded when he insisted on using a sheet to parachute off the Kilgos' barn. We tried our best to convince him not to jump—yep, wounded again! While playing football in the Sansburys' large front yard, Punk informed me he was going to "rack" me. I was not quite sure what that meant but quickly responded, "Go ahead." He tackled me full force and then immediately fell to the ground in agony, screaming. Barbara Welch, Clevie, Vera, Polly, and I watched, amazed at his despair. Since this was the second time he had broken his collarbone, I did not have full bragging rights! Bimmy sure had a skill I always admired. He could be talking to you, and *Bam*! Standing flatfooted, he could flip over in the air, landing right back on his feet before his sentence was completed. Bet he can still perform that trick today.

The Bonnoitt family was ahead of their time. They had a small, shallow in-ground pool in their backyard. We also enjoyed their trampoline and basketball court. Much to our surprise, they had a pet fox that screamed like a girl in distress. That sound took us to our knees—it just plain scared my mother, Cyndie, and me to death! You know Noni had a wonderful way of telling stories, and I can still hear her fabulous little giggle. She just bubbled over when that captivating smile spread across her face. Every time I looked up, she was pulling in her driveway with a gallon of milk and a loaf of bread. Her kids inhaled her supply. I'm not sure what I did to Linda Bonnoitt, but it must have been bad because she pinned me down on the ground in my own front yard and worked up a slow long spit. Sure enough, it landed right between my eyes! Sandra was the oldest of the four kids. She became a nurse and offered to be my delivery coach when I gave birth to our daughter, Lezlie, in 1975. Having Sandra with me was a real gift (another lifelong friendship)! I have to say, the Bonnoitt house was always busy and full of energy.

Stan Drawdy

Business Education

O ne good thing about living in a neighborhood with lots of kids
is it means you have lots of things to do and lots of people to
play with and to learn from. Two of the older kids who seemed to
understand the most about the business world were Tom Dewitt
and Jimbo Brown. Out of all the kids in the neighborhood, I'd say
that these two were the first to teach the rest of us kids about the
business world. Or at least they were the first to teach me lessons
about business.

Tom was a good bit older than me, but his brother Jim and I
were close to the same age, and I was often at the Dewitts' house with
Jim. Tom was very impressive to me for several reasons. First of all, he
played on the high school football team…either JV, varsity, or maybe
both, I don't remember; but I do remember seeing him dressed and
heading to practice or coming home from practice. For the first three
years that we lived on Greenway Drive, the Dewitts lived next door.
They had the house at the very end of the street, where it turned into
a dirt road and made a circle before coming back onto the paved road.

The second reason I was impressed by Tom was he had a jar
of money in his room. Jim told me that Tom always had money
because he had a paper route and sold subscriptions for the newspaper. Tom was the only kid I knew that had a real job and was still
just a kid. And how cool was that to have a jar full of money saved
up in your room that you could get to whenever you needed it. And
the third impression that Tom made on me was MONOPOLY. Tom
Dewitt introduced me to the greatest board game ever invented…

Monopoly. I fell in love with that game, and the very next Christmas, I got Santa to bring me my very own game.

I believe that many people developed a foundation for the housing business because of the principles and ideas learned in that game. Tom was a master at the game, and by observing his strategy, I became quite good at it myself. The idea is to invest in all the properties you can, negotiate with anyone you can to obtain their properties, improve the properties with structures such as houses and hotels, and then sit back and collect rent. That's when I learned about passive income, before I even knew there was such a thing. And I learned to save from seeing Tom's money jar and realizing if you saved money, then you would always have something to fall back on during hard times. Mom always called it "rainy days." I soon copied Tom's idea about a cash jar…still have one to this day.

Oftentimes, kids on Greenway Drive would try their hands at business. I've seen many lemonade stands come and go. And I have to admit that I tried my share of businesses when I lived on Greenway Drive. I learned a lot from each of my startup businesses. Johnny and I learned that quartz is worthless, when we started our mining business. Punk and I learned that not too many people wanted to come to our concert when we did our interpretation of the Beatles and that a utility trailer does not make a good stage unless you block it up on both ends, to keep it from flipping over. I also learned that buying items to sell requires that you are able to get them at wholesale prices if you want to make a profit. There was one business on Greenway Drive that was to a kid's business what Walmart is to dime stores. And just like Walmart, it put most other kid businesses to shame and out of business. It was the casino!

Jimbo Brown was the other entrepreneur kid in the neighborhood. Jimbo was older than me also and way smarter when it involved business. He owned and operated the best business ever on Greenway Drive. We called it Jimbo's Casino, and it was open every summer for several years. The Browns had a screened-in porch on the side of their house, and that's where the casino was located. As I recall, there was a utility room off the back of the porch-casino that had a chest freezer, and inside the chest freezer was the infamous product that Jimbo developed. It was the signature product of Jimbo's Casino. You could buy them, or you could win at the game venues of the casino. Yes, I am talking about cupsicles. Every kid on the street had a version of the cupsicle in their freezer at home. Some made them in ice trays. Some had store-bought containers with sticks like real popsicles, but no one had ever thought to put Kool-Aid in a small Dixie cup and then freeze them. The ones frozen in the Dixie cup were ten times better than those Mom made in her ice tray. And you could only get them at Jimbo's Casino.

The casino was an awesome idea, and all the neighborhood kids were drawn to it. I do not remember all the games available for pay-to-play, but I do remember a few of them. There was a ping-pong table, and you could play singles or doubles. Then he had a roulette wheel. There were also card games to play. But everyone's favorite was the putt-putt golf game. A hole in one would get you a cupsicle. Most of the time, we would play putt-putt till we got down to our last dime. Then Jimbo would sell us a cupsicle for our last ten cents. Going to Jimbo's Casino was always a fun time.

As I think about the kids on Greenway Drive and look at how most of us turned out in the real adult world, I would say that most became successful at their chosen profession. I can think of some who became teachers, coaches, lawyers, medical professionals, and then others who became business professionals or even started and ran their own businesses. I can't help but think that maybe…just maybe, Tom's Monopoly board and Jimbo's Casino had a small part in our successes.

We Called Him Coach

Greenway Drive was home to many important men in the town of Darlington, South Carolina. There were men from many walks of life. There were two well-known attorneys, two school principals (my dad was one), and two football coaches. We had a couple of car dealers, a building contractor, a pharmacist, a mailman, a couple of business owners, a salesman, and a military guy. How fortunate I was to grow up with so many positive role models. These men were not just leaders of their families but were strong leaders in the community. Most of the men were also close friends with my dad, Harvey Drawdy. Mr. Brown lived next door, and he once loaned us a truck camper, and we used it on a family vacation in the Smoky Mountains and Tennessee. Dad hunted and fished a lot with Robert Mills and Kenneth Bryant. I'd say that Kenneth was Dad's best friend because they were always doing fun things like hunting, fishing, cooking stews, robbing beehives, or working on motors. The good thing about being a son is that you kinda automatically get to do some of the fun things that your dad does. Kenneth Bryant was our next-door neighbor, and next to my dad was probably the closest adult friend whom I had on Greenway Drive.

As I think back and reflect on all the great men of Greenway Drive, I can honestly say that almost every one of them had an influence on my life in some positive way, and I am grateful for each one. However, one man who lived on the street was very special to me and someone whom I tried to pattern my adult life after.

I think the first time I met Coach Welch was through my dad. Dad and Coach were friends and colleagues, both working for Darlington area schools. I think they both were part of a men's group that occasionally met at the old Mineral Springs Park for cookouts and fellowship. They had also been fishing together at Coach Welch's cabin on the river at White Oak. Dad also helped Coach Welch with the athletic program, first as a JV coach and then as the manager of ticket sales at all athletic events. At some point, I was with Dad, and he introduced me to Coach. Every boy in the neighborhood talked and dreamed about playing football for Coach Welch and the Blue Devils. I was no exception.

Wayne Howle lived across the street from Coach Welch. Wayne was a year older than me, but we often played football together in his front yard. We both had shoulder pads and helmets, and we would put those on to play. Wayne had a Washington Redskin set that he won in the Punt, Pass, and Kick Contest, which was so cool. My equipment must have come from Santa Claus. Wayne also had a nice football jersey, and I had one of Harvey's old T-shirts covering my pads. But the point is we played one-on-one, mano a mano, full gear, full dress-up football. It was always the Washington Redskins versus whoever I wanted to be in Dad's old T-shirt!

Wayne had another cool thing in his yard…a two-by-four nailed between two pine trees behind his house that made a great goal post, eight to ten feet high. It was perfect for practicing field goals. Wayne was good at kicking the ball over the crossbar, but I never quite mastered that technique.

On one of the early fall days that I was playing at Wayne's house, we had concluded our game, and I was walking home, which was only about a hundred yards up the street. A car pulled up and stopped. It was Coach Welch. At first, I thought I had done something wrong, and it made me nervous. When he rolled his window down, I noticed that he had a whistle hanging around his neck, so I figured he was getting home from practice. He said to me, "You are Harvey's boy, aren't you?" I said, "Yes, sir." Then he said, "When you get to high school, you can play for me." Then he drove down the road. I turned and watched till he turned left into his driveway. Then I ran the rest of the way to my house. The high school football coach had just stopped and spoken to me and asked me to play for the Blue Devils. That had always been my dream and goal, and now it seemed real and possible. That may have been the day that football became my favorite sport. That may have been the day that I stamped my ticket for the journey of a lifetime. That may very well have been the day that started my love affair with football, not as a player but as a high school coach for over thirty years.

Over the next ten to twenty years, I watched and admired Coach Welch. Dad took me to all the home varsity and JV games. Some of the older boys in the neighborhood were already playing on the high school team for Coach Welch. I couldn't wait for my chance to be a Blue Devil. By the time I became old enough to play for St. John's High at any level, my family had moved away from Greenway Drive. Mom and Dad had built their dream home on five acres of land out in the country. I had just finished the seventh grade when we moved into that house, where my parents still live today.

I was able to reunite with my Greenway Drive friends at school and with Coach Welch when I started playing JV football as a ninth grader. Many of the guys from Greenway Drive had played or were still playing for the St. John's Blue Devils when I joined the team. The ones whom I remember playing varsity or JV during my four years were Johnny, Steve, Punk, Bimmy, Danny, Pete, Jeff, Bobby, Mike, and Ricky. They were all good players and contributed to the success of the Blue Devils football team. There were many others from the neighborhood who played before and after my four years.

St. John's High football coach Jimmy Welch
and the quarterback Stan Drawdy.

At some point, we all got to know Coach Welch as one of his players. It was during those years that I really got to know Coach on a personal level. I had already experienced the strong, stern, dignified side of Coach. The side of him that commanded respect and admiration. The side that made me want to be like him. He was a great role model for those of us who played for him. As a player and later as an assistant coach, I was able to see the caring, compassionate, and humorous side of Coach Welch. That was the side that made him such a good friend.

In 2019, Coach Welch was inducted into the South Carolina Athletic Coaches Association Hall of Fame. It was such an honor for me to be a part of that ceremony and to be able to tell how important Coach Welch was to so many of the young men who grew up in Darlington…especially to those of us on Greenway Drive. What a blessing he was and still is to those of us who called him "Coach."

Peggy Melton Greene

Fond Memories
from the Babysitter

L et me share a few things that I can remember about each one
of the precious little children on Greenway Drive and close by.
As well as I can remember at eighty years old, I started babysitting
when I was almost twelve years old. David Brown was my first job.
Then before too long, I started babysitting his cousins, Robbie and
Jimbo. Word got out, I think, that I only charged twenty-five cents
an hour regardless of how many children were in the family. Also,
that I played harder than they did while there. (It is called loving
what you do!) Very soon, I had acquired another job keeping the
three Truluck children; next came the Smyre children, who lived near
the Paul Sansbury kids. Then, lo and behold, my high school football
coach Welch's daughter Barbara. (Wow!) Then came my high school
principal Bill Cain and Mrs. Cain, with their two children, Sarah and
Bill. I always had to search the neighborhood trying to locate them
before I could keep them! How very embarrassing—"Your High
School Principal!"

Another precious little girl who lived close by was Susan
Johnson, whose mother was one of the most outstanding nurses in
the city, Dot Johnson. I even babysat the child of the track coach,
Bruce Lynch! Cool! Somehow, I ventured out and took another customer up the hill, David Cohen's baby. I do not know—that poor
little baby must have been afraid of me. He NEVER stopped crying,

and I would cry too. I continued to charge only twenty-five cents, and I think this probably was the reason business was booming!

Let me share a few things that I remember about each one of their darling little children. David Brown—he loved for me to keep him. He stuck to me like glue, and he would cry and cry when I had to go home. Once when I was keeping him, my grandmother died. He cried so hard his mother had to let him go with me to my grandmother's house. He was a very sweet little guy, and I think he knew that he was special, and he was! Robbie Brown—she would corner me the minute her parents left the house with all these questions; she would not ask the parents: "Peggy, how old do I have to be before I can wear a bra?" "What should I do with my hair?" "When will the boys start liking me?" Meanwhile, her little brother Jimbo, who was trying to see through the snowstorm on the TV, kept asking me "Could I please clear up the picture?" "Could I see anything or anybody on it?" If so, "Who is it?"

Well, I soon received a call—could I babysit the three little Truluck children? I loved to sit with them. They were all so happy and fun to keep. Barbara had a collection of little dolls with hair that could be changed around and redressed. She wanted to try on my red lipstick. Of course, I let her. She was an extremely happy, happy, happy little girl. Her brother Johnny loved to hide from me, pretending to have left the house! He was very good at this, and it would really put me to the test (scary)! The other brother, Ingram, loved to catch snakes from the stream down in the woods behind their house. Once when I was there, he came flying into the room with his empty shoebox (the snake cage), saying his snake had escaped, somewhere in the house! Could I please help him find it? I said, "That's it, I'm gone, see you!" I'm scared to death of snakes!

It was little Susan Johnson. I do not know why, but she had this compulsion to strip out of her clothes (three years old)! The dead of winter—she raced outside to her swings and swung! Even when her mother pinned her clothes on, she still would manage to get out of them. She would also climb over the back fence to the neighbor's house and turn on the water hose. The neighbor would come running out, and Susan would turn the hose on her! Pretty funny, she moved like lightning.

I babysat the Paul and Mary Anne Sansbury children, Clevie and Andy. Clevie was an extremely quiet child but also extremely busy. You really had to keep your eye on her. Andy was entertained by his sister's actions. The high school band director and his wife, Eloise, had three children—they were angelic. So easy to keep, extremely calm, and cooperative, very easy! I finally got another regular job, working after school and on the weekends at Wilson Clinic. I had planned to go to a nurses' school after graduation. Therefore, I was not available to babysit any longer.

In closing, as you can see, I have fond memories of all these wonderful young people. I am proud of the way they have all turned out, to be very productive people, and they are now wonderful parents. I am grateful for this opportunity to share my small contribution to their lives. They will always have a place in my heart.

Keith Carter

Furniture on the Roof

P eggy Melton was the "big girl" in my life when I was a pre-schooler. My memory is that she was a very pretty teenager who lived around the corner from us on Spring Street, and that on a couple of occasions, she helped my mother by providing babysitting services, possibly beginning after my sister Shelley was born, when I was three and a half. My mother was acquainted with Peggy's mother, Mrs. Melton, and thought highly of her and Peggy. The day after Halloween in the mid-1950s, Mrs. Melton was talking to my mother about the shenanigans that had been played on her house the night before. She said they were not at home to give out candy, and it was clear that somebody really believed in the "TRICK" part of trick-or-treating. She didn't discover the tricks until the next morning. It turns out that some "boys" (and how she knew it was boys was not hard to figure out) had placed all of the Meltons' yard furniture on the roof! The problem was how to get it down! Mrs. Melton didn't have a ladder or any other way to get the furniture off her roof, and I don't know what the answer was. She also said that her window screens were "soaped," which was a practice akin to the "TP-ing" stunt that became popular some years later. For those not familiar with soaping, a bar of soap was used to write, draw, or mark on window screens. It was quick and easy to do but very unquick and uneasy to remove.

My mother instantly recognized the focus of these antics— no one hated Mrs. Melton, but someone really liked Peggy! Some boy(s) who desired her attention and favor had pulled the pranks,

169

not knowing any other way to get her attention. I learned a few years later that this was, indeed, a dilemma for a boy who liked a girl but was too shy, dumb, and inexperienced to actually approach her and let her know it in a positive way. It has always been a problem, and the result has been many absurd antics which usually resulted in the very opposite reaction than the one desired. Peggy very likely knew or had a good idea who had done the deeds and may have told her mother but only if she didn't care for the boy, is my guess. Only she knows the answer, if she even remembers it!

Danny Sansbury

My Mama to the Rescue (Again)

It was Labor Day Monday, which was always a big deal in Darlington. After all, our hometown hosted the Southern 500 race every Labor Day. That race put our small town on the national map. To this day, whenever I travel anywhere, people recognize the name of "Darlington" from "the race."

That particular Labor Day Monday was the morning after the passing of Hurricane Dora in 1964. Overnight, the heavy rains had flooded the Dewitt ponds at the end of our street. The small earthen dams had given way, and the ponds had emptied into the small creek that ran behind the Trulucks' house, all the way down to Williamson Park. The creek flowed under the bridge on Spring Street and then split into three branches as it made its way through the park.

Word soon spread through our neighborhood that Jim Dewitt and Johnny Truluck were in a wooden johnboat floating down the creek toward the park. Many of us raced to the bridge to welcome their arrival. Darrell Newsome was also with me, as he had spent the previous night at our house. When we got to the bridge, we stared back into the swampy area behind the Brasingtons' home. That was where the swollen current would inevitably bring the johnboat. As children, we had not thought about how the floodwaters racing under the bridge and into the park had the power to suck the boat sideways and pull both boat and boys under the bridge to some bad end. Someone had alerted my mother what was happening, and she hastily followed us to the bridge. While we merely stared at the growing peril, my mother intervened. A qualified water-safety instructor, she taught Red Cross swimming classes every summer to children and adults alike. She constantly schooled us in water safety. Only she realized that this adventure had great danger attached to it.

At the moment the johnboat was forcibly turned sideways and tipped so as to throw both boys into the floodwaters being squeezed under the bridge, my mother reached down and simultaneously pulled both boys out of the boat and onto the bridge to safety. What strength it took to lift two thirteen- or fourteen-year-olds at the same time! The boat disappeared under the bridge. What could have been a terribly tragic accident instead became another Greenway Drive adventure to be remembered all these years later.

Onlookers at Swift Creek Bridge, Spring Street,
observing the very high waters.
From front to back: Clevie Sansbury, Susie Sansbury, Fran Wall,
Danny Sansbury, Andy Sansbury, and Judy Scott (standing).

What happened next, though, was just as amazing to us children. Mama invited all who wanted to do so to get on their bathing suits and ride out to the Darlington Country Club, where Black Creek meandered beside several holes on the golf course. Mama drove our 1961 blue-and-white Plymouth station wagon. A record nineteen people (one adult driver, eighteen children) were crowded into it. We parked near old #1 hole, which is now #13.

That day, Black Creek no longer wandered around the golf holes. It went more or less straight across. We walked down the fairway to the tee box of old #2, a par 3 hole. Some of us swam out to the green. We then went to the swimming area around the bend. My mother, the water-safety instructor, supervised our swimming in the dark water.

I cannot help but think how reckless this behavior would seem to cautious parents today. For us, it was a temporary delight in flooded waters on a hot Labor Day.

The amazing day was still not over! That afternoon, some of us returned to what remained of the Dewitt ponds. There we saw surviving fish now limited to small shallow puddles. Word had gone out that Mr. Drawdy would prepare a fish fry for the neighborhood if we caught enough fish. There in the mud we grabbed the fish by hand, put them into buckets, and delivered the buckets of fish to the Drawdys' house. When I got back home, Mama took one look at Andy and me and refused to let us into her clean house! She made us stand in the yard and hosed us off until she had gotten the worst of the mud off of us.

A few weeks later, Mr. Drawdy served a fish fry to the neighborhood at the picnic area at Mineral Springs.

Andy and the Alligator

There were many times that a group of us were playing in our open front yard. On this particular morning, Thelma Wall pulled up to the side of the yard. She called to us to tell us that she had just come back from the grocery store. She told us that she had just seen a small alligator at the intersection of Evans Circle and Spring Street. All of us bolted down the street to see the gator. We ran past the Scotts' house on the left and the Walls', Pates' and Brasingtons' homes on the right. My brother Andy stopped in our garage to get the snake-catching tool that my mother had crafted. Andy brought the tool with him, for he intended to catch the gator.

With all of us staring at the rather small gator, he was frozen in place. Andy slipped up behind him and got the noose around his head. Andy then picked the gator up and brought him to our house. We put him in the wooden box used from time to time to keep snakes. We kept this gator for over a week like a house pet. Sometimes, he was calm, almost friendly, and would allow you to hold him. Other times, he had a pretty nasty disposition.

A week later, we took the gator to the lifeguard at the swimming pool at the Country Club. When his shift was over that afternoon, he took the gator down to Black Creek and let him go.

Andy Sansbury and an alligator.

174

Merle Drawdy

Biters Gonna Bite

When the weather was nice and warm, Greenway Drive would come alive! Kids would be playing; dogs barking; birds chirping; and us stroller moms pushing those buggies up and down the street, carrying our toddlers, getting some exercise and sun. As we pushed those little bundles of joy, we also had to keep an eye out for our slightly older children, who were usually walking along with us, vying for a bit of Mom's attention too. Everyone knew each other, and it was common for several of us mothers to be strolling along together, or even stopping off in one of the mom's yards just to chat a bit, mostly about our husbands or our kids, but sometimes laughing, sometimes complaining, and, of course, catching up on the gossip when necessary. Those were truly great times and now great memories.

My Ricky was a toddler, maybe three years old at the time, and what us mothers referred to as "a biter." I had to watch him closely, or he would find a way to bite one of the other children. Punishment was no stranger to him, but for some reason, the spankings and punishments just did not sink in enough to change his behavior. Ricky had to be watched closely. I remember one particular day, a group of us moms were out doing our walking and talking and truly not paying attention...not good! I looked up, and Ricky was wide-open chasing another little boy, Brent Sansbury. Brent's parents were some of the kindest people you would ever know, and Brent had developed the same sweetness and kindness of his family, and now my little biting son was stalking and chasing sweet little Brent, like a cheetah after a gazelle.

Ricky was in full chase mode after poor little Brent, reason unknown. I literally freaked out! Then I took off after Ricky, screaming his name as loudly as I could, hoping to stop him in his tracks, to no avail. By the time I got to him, Ricky had Brent on the ground and was biting him on his tiny face. I was ready to die! My child, my blood kin, had hurt this precious child of Dot and Howard Sansbury. It was awful. Brent was crying, I was crying, Ricky was crying, I felt awful, and by now I was hysterical. I was expecting the wrath of an angry mom to be upon me, and deservedly so, but what I saw was a calm passionate mother. Sweet Dot picked up her child, telling him and me that he was okay and that everything would be all right. Thank You, dear Heavenly Father, the bite was not as bad as it first seemed. It was mostly bruised and not as bad as it could have been. His mom took him to the doctor to be checked, and the treatment was a tetanus shot and bandage.

Dot was not angry at me or at Ricky. We became very good friends. Rick and Brent played together for many years, and Ricky never bit him again.

But the story does not end there. Ricky's next victim was one of Lottie and Kenneth's girls, Patricia Bryant. They lived next door to us after we moved to our second house on Greenway Drive. Ricky and Patricia were playing between our two houses. The play turned to arguing, then to fighting. Ironically, Patricia was also "a biter..." Both began biting each other and snapping at one another. Both were screaming, and by the time I got to them, Lottie had snatched Ricky up and was screaming at him and at me while pushing him away from her daughter. I got upset at Lottie for the way she was treating my son. Then she and I had words with each other. I snatched Ricky from her arms, spanked him for biting, and then took him in the house. Lottie and I didn't speak for several days, but soon it passed, and we made up. But the biting was too serious, so I had to get control of it. The biting had to stop. From that day forward, if Ricky even looked like he was thinking about biting, he got a whipping. Soon he got the message, and the biting stopped.

Life became better for us all! Lottie and I could literally stand in our kitchens with the side doors open and talk to each other.

That's how close the houses were to each other. Lottie and I became best friends. Harvey and Kenneth became best friends as well. We were all very close. We took vacations together and laughed together and cried together. They became like family, and her kids were my kids, and mine were hers. I miss Lottie. She was truly my BFF (best friend forever).

Ingram Truluck

Field Trips with Mr. Cain

Two O'clock in the Morning!

B ack when I was eight or nine years old, I didn't think of Mr. Cain as a school principal. I thought of him as Billy's dad. And Sarah's dad. He was the high school principal, but that was unknown territory for a kid. Billy Cain and I were in the same grade at St. John's Elementary, and for the first several years of my life the Cains lived just across the street from us on Greenway Drive, up on the hill and almost out of sight. Our house had been the fourth house on the right from Spring Street, but then we moved into our new house down by the curve on Greenway.

I don't remember how the invitation was given, but I was invited to spend the night with Billy. And not just spend the night with him, but his dad wanted to take us to Charlotte. And not just go to Charlotte, but to go to an ice hockey game! The whole idea was out of this world for me! I had never been out of South Carolina before! My mother was from Anderson and we went there sometimes, but that was still in South Carolina. Charlotte was in North Carolina, and it was a mighty big deal!

And go to an ice hockey game? I knew what ice was, but ice hockey? I thought I knew what hockey was too, but it wasn't a game. It was much later that I learned that Charlotte had just gotten an ice hockey team, but that wasn't big news around Darlington. Mr. Cain knew things that most dads didn't know nor care about. For Mr. and Mrs. Cain, education was their job, and gardening was their hobby.

I knew that Billy and Sarah were often busy with chores around the yard, and then they had to study and do homework a lot. My life was not nearly as structured. But we had a lot of fun when we did play—Billy and me.

So, the deal was that I would join Billy and Mr. Cain for a car trip out of state, and after the game we would come back to his house and I would spend the night there. That part wasn't very odd. Sleeping happened every night, and one place was as good as another, but the idea was still fun. But this was all new and different. I had no idea what it would be like to ride to Charlotte. And to go to a game called ice hockey. I was excited and looked forward to it. That afternoon, and it had to have been a Friday, I walked up the street to the Cains' house with a bag with my toothbrush in it.

It was just us three guys—Mr. Cain, Billy, and me. Billy and I didn't pay any attention to where we were going; we just rode, talked about football and fishing and building forts on the Cain's property. They had more than just a lot with a front and back yard. They had all kinds of things: trees, fields, bushes, hills. It seemed huge to me. We rode and we talked.

Mr. Cain told us when we were coming to the state line between South Carolina and North Carolina. We looked out then, but Billy had been out of state before. I looked to see what the differences would be. I noticed it was a little hillier than home, but not that much different. There were more houses and buildings than we had. We quit looking, but after a while Mr. Cain said, "We're coming into Charlotte." We started looking hard then, especially me. It was a city, not a town. There were lots of cars and trucks, and finally Mr. Cain said, "Boys, up ahead is the Charlotte Coliseum!" We gazed through the windshield and saw the shiny, round, silver dome. It was like nothing I had ever seen before! As we got closer, it got bigger and bigger! I was speechless. This Charlotte was very fancy!

Going into the Coliseum and finding our seats was a blur, now that I think back. It was all so stupendous and new that I couldn't even think about it. There were more people in there than I had ever seen at one time. The football and basketball games we went to at St. John's were big stuff, I had thought. This was so much bigger that

179

it didn't mean anything. It was just way bigger stuff! The court was white as snow, and Mr. Cain told us that was the ice where the game would be played. When the players came out on ice skates and started skating around in circles, and a very loud horn would blow a lot, it was more than I could figure out. I didn't really try. I never did understand what they were doing since it was unlike any game I had ever seen before. Several times everybody jumped up and cheered, and the players were very happy, so I knew they had scored. I remember very little about it other than the noise and the big pictures in my mind.

I guess we got something to eat at some point, but I didn't care about that. I'm sure I told my parents all about it later, but now I've forgotten most of it. The most exciting thing of all was yet to come!

When the game ended and we made our way to the car in the parking lot, it was already past my usual bedtime. I had no idea what time it was, but I sure felt sleepy. Billy and I both dozed off in the backseat very soon after Mr. Cain started driving. I didn't know anything until Mr. Cain woke us both up as we were coming down the Spring Street hill. What? Where was I? What was going on? It took me a few seconds to come out of a sound sleep just as we pulled into the Cains' driveway. By the time we climbed out of the car into the chilly night air, I was wide awake. I was still spending the night with Billy!

There was no noise. None! No cars, no people anywhere, no nothing. Just black night. Mr. Cain said, "All right, boys, it's very late and we have to get to bed right away. It's two o'clock in the morning."

Two o'clock in the morning! What? "No wonder everything feels so strange," I thought! I had heard about times like that—times during the night—but I didn't know that everything still existed during the night. I had never been awake even to twelve o'clock at night, and surely not in the morning when it was still black night! I had the strange sensation that I was in another world since nobody else in the world was awake but us.

We went right on to bed pretty soon after that. I remember feeling very funny and sleepy. Later I thought about it. I had ridden to Charlotte, in North Carolina. I had been inside the big silver spaceship, where there was an ice hockey game with lots of people. There was a lot of noise and confusion, horns and yelling. But none of that could touch the fact that I was actually up and walking around at two o'clock in the morning! In the middle of the night! That was unreal, and spooky. And I lived to tell about it!

Gaddy's Goose Pond

Mr. Cain invited me to go with his family to North Carolina again. This time Mrs. Cain and Sarah also went, along with Billy and me. It was a Saturday morning, and Mr. Cain told us as we drove out of Darlington that we were going to a place in North Carolina where a man named Mr. Gaddy had been feeding "Canadian geese" for years as they migrated. Now a whole lot of them stopped over every year and spent a night or two, eating, and swimming in Mr. Gaddy's pond. It was quite a thing, Mr. Cain told us. I had seen pictures of a goose or two in books, but I had not actually seen one in person. Mr. Cain told us that Canadian geese aren't white like most book geese, but are grey and black. And when they fly, they form into a vee shape. He said it was exciting to see. He said we could even feed them. He was always teaching, and Mrs. Cain too; they told us that Mr. Gaddy could recognize a lot of the geese year after year, and that he was their good friend.

As we drove out of Darlington on North Main Street, Mr. Cain told us that we were on Highway 52, and that we would not make a single turn on our trip, until we turned into Mr. Gaddy's farm which is also on Highway 52 in North Carolina. That made the trip sound like a short one, but it was almost as long as the drive to Charlotte that he took us on.

Again, I don't have many specific memories of the trip or the goose pond, but I do remember seeing a lot of geese and a lot of people. When we turned into his place, there were cars parked everywhere—all over the fields and yard as far as we could see. A lot of people wanted to see and feed the geese from Canada, which were unusual sights for everybody back then. I know I was seeing them for the first time. Geese were constantly flying in and landing on the pond. To make room, other geese got up and flew away. A lot more were walking around. I do remember that we had to be careful where we stepped!

Now we are all very familiar with Canada geese, which are with us all year around. They dropped in for a stopover on their travels, thanks to Mr. Gaddy, and the word got out all over Canada—they decided to stay! It seems to happen with a lot of Northern visitors!

Fran Wall Weaver

Our Neighborhood Part 4

Mary Ruth Brasington and Vera

What a blessing I received when the Brasington family moved from Pinehaven to Evans Circle. Vera was ten years old. While I was on Greenway Drive, we had lived diagonally as backdoor neighbors when we were two and a half years old (just days apart). The Brasingtons had a large family—Mary Ruth and Bill with kids Vera, Polly, Wanda, and Billy. Bill's dad also lived with the family, and he could not hear well, so the TV was always playing very loudly in the home. Mary Ruth was beautiful with her high cheekbones, olive skin, dark hair, and dark eyes. She looked like the British actor Audrey Hepburn, and she dressed like her too. She was strong and very brave, and while ill, she always repeated the twenty-third Psalm. I memorized it under her influence. She had high expectations about life and living it abundantly. While spending many hours with her, I always knew there was a sweet spirit in her, and I still miss her. At one time, she had managed the UFO-looking Southernaire Restaurant in Darlington, and many of us teens from the neighborhood enjoyed fun parties held there, upstairs in the dome. We also liked driving around and around the circular building.

Mary Ruth had strict rules for us to follow: "Don't Ever Stand on the Sidewalk with a Soda Bottle in Your Hand." It Just Was Not Ladylike! Vera was amazing! Being the oldest, she could care for her mother, assist the younger children with their homework, make fabulous grades herself, and was a heck-of-a-defensive basketball player.

She drove all of us to each school. I usually made them late. Most days after completing their homework, Polly, Wanda, and Billy were out of the house like a bullet. One of Polly's favorite activities was fishing. She could collect her bait and grab a pole along with a can of boiled peanuts, and before you knew it, she had a stringer full of fish. She is still a fisherwoman! Stunning little Wanda was our social butterfly and was off to play with Judy Scott and Nancy Powers or headed to Pinehaven to see her fun-loving aunt Joanne and play with her cousin Lynn (Strictly Girl Stuff). Billy Boy was a master engineer. Sometimes, he would replace his bike's handlebars with the lawn-mower handle. We were amazed he did not wreck while riding with his hands over his head. Abracadabra, you just never knew what his next design would be.

But my fondest memory is of Vera standing in front of the stove cooking where she made tasty dinners each night, with a favorite being country-style steak and gravy with all of the fixings. She would cook with her right hand, all while holding a book and reading from her left. Talk about multitasking—she was a pro, a hero for all, and she continues to be precious always. I did contribute a little by setting the table and getting the drinks ready. I also stole and ate the pickled onions out of her dad Bill's sweet pickle jar. He would notice and give me a little crooked smile when he got back into town from his weeklong, over-the-road hauls for Dixie. He was fun and shared his wooden crates of empty soda bottles to cash in for our party supplies. I cherish the blessed days I've shared with my forever, loving, and inspirational friend—Vera.

Our Own Southern 500 Parade and Race

Vera's uncle, Harold Brasington, designed the Darlington Raceway. He bought the land from Mr. Ramsey, and since the pond was not included in the sale, the shape of the track had to be a bit oval/egg shaped (The Track Too Tough to Tame). That track could not even compare to our Labor Day Southern 500 parade and races on Greenway Drive. We did not need stock cars; we had hand-painted model cars that were decaled for specific drivers (Fireball Roberts,

Junior Johnson, Richard Petty). And there were bicycle races with streamers and playing cards clothes-pinned on the spokes creating race-like sound effects. I can still see Pete and Jeff Sansbury flying down the fence line alongside Brent Sansbury's yard now. Their dad sold cars, so they knew all about putting your foot to the pedal. We created a First Aid Station to patch up our drivers after blowouts and wipeouts. Oh no, here comes the Mercurochrome and Merthiolate with their glass-tube applicators where we would tell the person applying the burning topical antiseptic to "Blow-Blow-Blow." Also on standby were ice packs and Band-Aids. When we were young, sometimes our uncle Claud Smith would take Cyndie and me out to the racetrack to collect money from the sale of race tickets. He always had his weapon in his pocket and pulled right up close to the ticket office. There were many policemen and patrolmen out front. We stayed in the car. He'd go in, make the collection, and come out with a huge brown paper bag full of cash. We then drove downtown to C&S Bank to make the deposit. Cyndie and I had no clue we were decoys! We had been busy looking at the race fans. They took their car seats out of their cars and put them out on the grass, even in the ditches, and had a fine time living it up. We kids on Greenway Drive did not party like that.

Entertaining Ginny Pate

The Pate family lived beside the Brasingtons on Evans Circle. Ginny prepared her supper meal each day at lunchtime. She would fry up the mess of fish Ben had caught (or maybe some pork chops) and would place each piece of meat on individual slices of loaf bread to drain the grease. Now my conservative mother thought this act was very wasteful (unless they chowed down on the loaf bread along with the meal). Her motto was "Waste Not, Want Not!" With Ginny's dinner meal being prepared early in the day, she was available to spend most of her evenings at our house on Mother's kitchen chair/ stepstool. She loved to visit with us while Mama was preparing our nightly meal. Cyndie and I were addicted to her quick wit and her way with prose. She kept us in stitches with her stories. Ginny was our very own personal "Life of the Party." That little chair/stepstool now has a special place in the kitchen of the log cabin in Tryon, North Carolina, the town where Mother grew up! (It's not as much fun now without Ginny seated there).

Sammy Howell

I was always glad Sammy Howell had grown up in "the Hood." Especially so when I decided to take Mechanical Drawing in high school with our neighbor and instructor, Coach Bruce Lynch. I obviously did not study the syllabus, because I sure was not thrilled having to draw nuts and bolts. Sammy pretty much adopted me, drew his assignment, and then assisted with drawing mine too! I think Coach Lynch was lenient with me. Some years later, when I was in interior design school, I took a four-hour test out of the drafting class. Thank you, Sammy, for making it all possible.

Stan Drawdy

Keep on Truckin'

Summertime was always the greatest time of the year on Greenway Drive for several reasons. The biggest reason was NO SCHOOL! No school meant no homework, no shoes, no problems, sleeping until we woke up, and no alarms waking us. It was the best time of the year, except maybe for Christmas.

Another great thing about summer was being able to play outside all day, which we thought was good until air conditioning came along. It was hotter inside most houses than it was outside, so being outside all day didn't seem to be a punishment (like it appears to be now to my grandchildren).

We also had "the summer movie series." We bought tickets during the last few weeks of school each year. The local theater showed a morning movie at ten o'clock every Tuesday and Thursday morning during the summer. The theater was usually pretty packed because most parents thought those tickets were a cheap babysitter. Most of us kids either walked or rode bikes to the theater, then back home afterward. We usually got home just in time for lunch, which was usually a peanut butter and jelly sandwich and a Dixie cup full of Kool-Aid handed out through the back screen door. Lunch was eaten outside while sitting under the two giant oak trees in our front yard at 112 Greenway Drive. There was usually at least one extra kid for lunch at the Drawdy house and occasionally several extras. Those were the best sandwiches, especially when Mom took time to cut off the crust and cut the sandwich so that it looked like a triangle.

Summertime was great on Greenway Drive. There was always some type of activity going on that made it almost impossible to get bored. And at the end of each day, there was always an event or two that just excited us kids more than one can imagine. Trucks, yes, trucks, would come rolling down the street. It was not an everyday occurrence, so you had to be on the lookout and listen out for them. The most popular one was the ice cream truck!

You could hear the ice cream truck coming. It played music—not popular music but ice cream truck music. This was way before people turned their cars into moving jukeboxes with bass sounds that rattle your windows. So when we heard music coming, we knew it was the ice cream truck. We could hear it as it rounded the curve on Spring Street at the top of the hill by Williamson Park. That gave us just enough time to sprint home and get ten cents from Mom and get back to where the truck would make its first stop. Ten cents would get you one soft serve cone, chocolate or vanilla, your choice! Usually, Mom would hand me a quarter and say, "Get Ricky one, and bring me my change." Now that meant I had to go get in line, buy the ice cream, walk back home, and then walk back to where all the kids were playing. But it was worth it to get the ice cream cone!

The second truck that we always looked forward to coming down Greenway Drive was like the stealth bomber. No warning sound, no big entrance, it just kinda appeared out of nowhere—the mosquito truck! The mosquito truck was an older model pickup owned by the town. It was black with rust and had a smoke-making machine in the bed. The smoke was a poison that spread out as the truck slowly puttered through the neighborhood, and the smoke killed gnats and mosquitoes. The good thing about the truck and the smoke was that we could run behind the truck and the smoke would be so thick you could hardly see, and the smoke didn't appear to kill kids. Of course, we often got fussed at for running behind the truck, but what else was a kid to do? It would be literally impossible to pass up that opportunity. Anyway, we were smart enough to hold our breath as we darted into and out of that smoke bomb.

There were other trucks that would come down our street that we also looked forward to. The garbage truck, the mail truck, and an occasional delivery truck were often seen; and those delivery trucks often conjured up curiosity among the kids and adults because everyone wondered what the delivery might have been. Also, we didn't get our milk and dairy products from the grocery store but rather from the milkman who drove the milk truck! We even had a milkman living in the neighborhood.

So it is an understatement to claim that trucking was a big deal to our neighborhood. Today, as more and more people order from the internet, trucking delivery services seem to be coming back, and even more important than they were in the 1950s and 1960s. Home delivery services seemed to have gone full circle over the last fifty to sixty years. Strange how the more things change, the more they stay the same! There was another truck that I always looked for on Greenway Drive. It was that old white 1960 pickup that my dad drove. Unlike the ice cream truck, the mosquito truck, the trash truck, milk truck, and delivery trucks that often came to our neighborhood, that old white pickup came home every day. Some days early, some days later, but it came home every day. How fortunate I was to have a dad who came home every day. To have a dad who comes home every day is a game changer for kids.

In today's society, things seem so divided and sometimes chaotic. Maybe if all of us men in this country took a stand to always be there for our kids, it might just make a difference. Until then, we will just keep on truckin'!

The Great Flood

There were several ponds located within the boundaries of what we considered to be our neighborhood. One of the ponds located at the far end of Greenway Drive was called Dr. Wilson's Pond because it was directly behind Dr. Wilson's small rental house that my family first lived in on Greenway Drive. Some say it was Dr. Wilson's office at one time. Attached to it was a smaller pond. We called it Dewitts' Pond because it was directly behind the house where the Dewitt family lived. Then there was a much smaller pond attached to Dewitts' Pond that we didn't really have a name for. I guess that was because it wasn't directly behind anyone's house. These three ponds formed a chain of ponds each one separated from the next one by a dam and a spillway that spilled water over into the next pond. So the no-name pond emptied into Dewitts' Pond, and then it emptied into Dr. Wilson's Pond. Dr. Wilson's Pond had a spillway that emptied into a tiny stream that ran along beside the Coach Lynch's house, then behind the Trulucks' and Coach Welch's, then finally emptied into Swift Creek. I called this creek Trulucks' Creek because that's the one we had to jump across to take the shortcut to Mr. Parnell's store.

Here are some important facts about the three ponds at the end of Greenway Drive. They were good for fishing, especially for bream and some catfish, and occasionally, you might hook into a nice-sized bass. Those ponds were also good for snake hunting. Ingram Truluck was the snake king among all of us kids, and I once saw him jump right into that pond and come out holding a big ole red-bellied water snake. Finally, if you walked across the dam between the no-name pond and Dewitts' Pond, it carried you out to Main Street. Turn right. and you were at Smith's Market, another store frequented by Greenway Drive kids. If you walked across the dam between Dewitts' Pond and Dr. Wilson's Pond, then keep going straight alongside the Muldrow house, and then straight across Main Street, you were only a "hop and a skip" away from Brunson-Dargan Junior High School. Behind the school was the football stadium and baseball stadium where the mighty Blue Devils played. There was also a tennis court behind there, but none of us cared much about that.

The second important body of water on Greenway Drive was Kilgos' Pond. It was the coolest pond because it was nestled back in the woods between the Kilgos' house and Pinehaven Avenue, a short avenue that was on the north side of Greenway Drive and runs parallel to the first half of Greenway Drive. Pinehaven was considered part of the neighborhood by most of us kids in those days. Actually, when we moved to Darlington from Great Falls, my parents had picked out a house on Pinehaven for us to rent. The night before we moved, the man called my parents and told them he had a chance to sell the house and he did and he was sorry but he couldn't turn down an offer to sell. That left the small Wilson house as the only place to get into before Dad started his new job teaching at the junior high school.

Here are some important facts about Kilgos' Pond. It had a fence around it. So that meant it was supposed to be off-limits. It had woods around it. That meant that it would be hard to see someone inside the fence. The fence had a washed-out place where the spillway ran down into the tiny creek. That created a gap under the fence big enough for a large kid to crawl through. I don't know for a fact, but rumor has it that the Kilgo Pond was full of giant bass and easy to catch with a broken-back Rebel lure or a Rapala. Another fact is that the creek it emptied into ran between the Browns' and the Howles' houses, down beside the Sansburys', and into Swift Creek. Swift Creek then ran through Williamson Park toward Black Creek.

That brings me to the third major body of water, Suggs' Pond. It was located directly across Spring Street from the entrance to Greenway Drive. It was a round-shaped pond, and it bordered Williamson Park. It actually spilled over into the park and into Swift Creek. Lots of people fished in that pond, but I never heard any stories about big fish there. I did know that there were some turtles living in that pond. One important thing about it was that people say it had gators in it too. Once a six-foot alligator was seen crossing Spring Street near the pond. Wildlife folks came out and caught it and carried it off.

They say that gators may have gotten there by people whose father went on a convention trip to Florida and brought his two sons baby gators. As the gators got too big to handle, the sons may have put them in Swift Creek. Gators love to eat turtles, so maybe they found their way into the pond searching for food.

Now that I have thoroughly explained how all the ponds are literally connected, because they all eventually empty into Swift Creek, I can explain the Great Flood of Greenway Drive. I do not remember the specific year that this occurred. I do not even know the exact time of the year that it occurred, but I think it was late spring or early summer. What I do know, without a doubt, is that this event occurred before Americans were made aware of global warming and climate change and that the weather conditions are not an act of God but rather caused by man's careless, selfish, and greedy use of natural resources and neglect of his environment. Back then, we all thought that weather disasters were caused by God and His friend, Mother Nature. After all, He did cause the whole world to flood even before fossil fuels were discovered. Regardless of who or what caused it, it started to rain really hard. Back then, one would say, "It's raining cats and dogs," or just simply "It is pouring down rain." For hours, it rained hard, then slowed, then hard again…creating heavy runoff water flowing into ponds and streams…

Today, they refer to it as "flash floods." It rained so hard and over a long enough period that all the ponds and streams filled up. And then it happened—the water in the three ponds at the end of Greenway Drive filled up so much that the dam between the no-name pond and Dewitts' Pond gave way, and all the water rushed into Dewitts' Pond. Then the next dam burst, and then Dr. Wilson's dam collapsed. All the water from those three ponds was rushing down the creek bed toward Swift Creek and Williamson Park. The rushing water literally created a river that was running right through Greenway Drive.

What I am about to tell you next is pure hearsay, but this is what I was told about two of Greenway Drive's most daring kids. I believe it was Jim and Johnny, but don't hold me to it. As the story goes, they saw what was happening and saw an opportunity of a lifetime. So they grabbed a boat, canoe, or raft; jumped in it; and went for the first and only white water rafting tour through the neighborhood. No paddles, no oars, just a wild ride through the ponds, over the dams, down the swollen streams, through the woods, and into a very high, swollen Swift Creek. They had no control over the speed or direction that the flood water was taking them and their vessel. As they hit Swift Creek headed for Williamson Park, they looked ahead and could see that the bridge on Spring Street had no space for them to get under. They abandoned ship! One of the boys swam to the edge, climbed out of the water, and turned around to see the other boy holding on to the huge pipe that crossed Swift Creek just in front of the bridge. With the help of an adult passing by on Spring Street, they were able to get him safely on shore. As far as the vessel in which the tour was made goes, it was last seen as it hit the bridge, was drawn underneath, and then popped up into the air on the other side of the bridge. To this day, it has never been found.

Clevie Sansbury Daniels

No One Plays Red Rover Anymore

O ur parents lived through the Great Depression and World War
II. Following the war, they began families and created the baby
boom. These were tough people, and they saw no reason to coddle
their children. Cars in the 1950s had no seat belts; the driver held
out the right arm (to catch flying kids) when applying the brake.
Our parents were tough; they expected that we could handle a bit of
heat or cold. My mother allowed us to throw sweet gum balls at each
other but not pine cones. We could learn to get out of the road when
a car was coming. We could learn not to touch poison ivy or pick up
poisonous snakes.

When our mothers yelled for us, we went home. Otherwise, we
were free within our Greenway Drive neighborhood to play. We had
lots of games—hopscotch, marbles, kickball, dodgeball, keep-away,
cops and robbers, king of the mountain, cowboys and Indians, army,
and all varieties of hide-and-seek-and-chase. My favorite game was
red rover. No one plays red rover anymore. It was a great game—two
sides, and you took turns trying to bust through the other team's
line. "Red rover, red rover, send Clevie right over." Oh, that was fun
to hear. I wanted to pick a spot to breach the line—hard enough to
be a challenge but not so hard that I would fail. Unfortunately, red
rover usually ended because at least one person was hurt. It was a
dangerous game, but it was fun.

We raised our children to be more careful. We had to know where they were—always. We became more fearful and raised them to see more danger in the world. No one plays red rover anymore.

Jim Brown

The Monster in the Barn

Summer days in a small Southern town are long and hot. As I walked out of my house, I saw David under the sycamore tree, doing tricks with his yo-yo.

"Whoa, new yo-yo!" I said.

"Yup. Duncan Imperial."

"Can you do 'Around the World?'" He sent the yo-yo spinning around his shoulder and deftly caught it when it completed its orbit.

"Cool," I said. I watched him play for a while and then said, "Well, what's on the agenda today?"

"I don't know," David said. He flipped the yo-yo a few more times and then put it in his pocket. "We could set up the ramps and jump bikes."

Jumping bikes was an activity we had begun last summer. We set up a couple of long flat boards at about a twenty-degree angle, facing each other, with a gap of about two feet between each of them. Then we would ride our bikes over the first board, jump the gap, and descend onto the other board. As the jumping progressed, we would space the boards farther apart and increase the angle by adding more bricks under the boards. Sometimes, we would start a fire in the gap with newspaper and sticks, and jump over the blaze. It made us feel like Evel Knievel.

"Nah, we already did that three times this summer," I said. Besides, I still had a sore knee from the last time we had jumped the ramps, when I had missed the exit board and crashed on the hard road. "How about getting some cherry bombs and making some humongous mudsplosions?"

A "mudsplosion" was created when high-powered fireworks were thrown into soupy mud, like the kind found in the pond behind Winky's house, when the dry summer months would cause the water level to fall. A well-thrown cherry bomb would result in an impressive explosion, provided it hit the surface at the precise time and the wet mud didn't extinguish the fuse. We would buy the cherry bombs and M-80's from a little store out on north Main Street, just out of town. No matter your age, a kid with money could buy anything there, including cigarettes and beer. "They're for Dad," was all you had to say.

"No, Dane and me and a couple of other kids did that last week," David said.

"What? Where was I?"

"You were at the movies."

"Oh yeah," I said. My sister and I had gone to see *War of the Worlds*. It scared the hell out of me. David and I were both silent for a while, thinking.

One thing was certain. Boredom was not an option.

"How about pulling the old 'Monster in the Barn' scam?" I said. "We haven't done that yet this year."

The Monster in the Barn was a hoax first perpetrated by two older boys in the neighborhood, Ingram and Leo. An old barn stood at the end of Greenway Drive. All the parents in the neighborhood forbid us to play around it, but, of course, we did. As a matter of fact, my sister Robbie had once broken her arm sliding off its tin roof. Anyway, the hoax worked like this. Leo would put on an apeman or Frankenstein mask and hide in the barn. Ingram would then spread the alarm that there was a monster in the barn. All the kids would rush to see the monster; and as they stood in a crowd outside the old structure, Leo would growl, kick the walls, and make other noises befitting a dangerous flesh-eating creature. Someone might dare a kid to enter the barn, and, of course, the kid would accept the dare. Then Leo would appear out of the shadows, roaring like a wild animal; and the kid would exit, screaming. Leo and Ingram had now grown too old to participate in the hoax, and it was left to us to continue the tradition and terrorize gullible children.

"Good idea," David said. "But let's get someone besides you or me to play the monster." Just then, Ingram's younger brother Johnny came riding by on his bicycle.

"Johnny! Come over here, man. We've got something cool for you to do."

Johnny listened to our proposal, and after bribing him with a bag of Sugar Babies I had left over from the movies, he agreed to play the monster. Now all we needed was a mask.

"Not me," said David.

"I don't have one either," said Johnny.

"Well, we'll figure out something," I said. We cut up strips of a wrinkled paper grocery bag and taped them to Johnny's face. Then we put Vaseline in his hair and slicked it back. The illusion should work in the darkened shadows of the barn.

"Now roar," said David. "Get really mad." Johnny roared.

"A perfect Wolfman," I said.

We sneaked Johnny down the street and into the barn without anyone seeing us. Then we set about spreading the alarm. Before long, a large crowd of wide-eyed kids had gathered. Some had even come from the adjoining neighborhood. Johnny did an Oscar-winning job, growling and beating on the walls. Each time a kid felt brave enough to enter the barn, he would shortly come out screaming; and that, of course, would provoke high-pitched wails of fear from the onlookers.

Everything was working out great until one of the toughest kids in the group announced, "I'll smoke that damn monster out," and I saw him reach into his pocket and pull out a cherry bomb. Before David or I could stop him, he rushed into the barn. A few seconds later, there was a loud boom, followed by an impressive string of curse words. The kid ran out of the barn, with the Wolfman close on his heels. Johnny tackled the kid and started punching his head and shoulders. As we pulled Johnny off, we heard the onlookers mutter, "Aw, heck, it's only Johnny," and "What a gyp." Slowly the crowd wandered off.

Luckily, Johnny was unhurt by the cherry bomb, and the kid who had thrown it went home with only a few bruises. But that was the last time we perpetrated the Great Monster in the Barn Hoax.

Harvey Drawdy

Friends Part 3

Kenneth and Lottie Bryant

After our move from the rental house to 112 Greenway Drive, my family became close friends with Kenneth, Lottie, Sandra, Patricia, and later, Kenny Bryant. Grady and Fran Greer sold us the little two-bedroom house, when they moved out to the Country Club. We lived there for the next six years. The Browns lived on one side of us and the Bryants on the other. Kenneth and I became lifelong friends, probably the closest friend of my life. Kenneth and I shared so many of the same interests. We fished, hunted, farmed, camped, played softball, cooked, and spent countless hours just hanging out together over the next sixty years. We were closer than brothers. My best friend passed away a couple of years ago, and part of me died with him. I miss him more than words can say, but I know that I will see him again because we also shared faith in Jesus Christ. That faith gives me comfort and assurance that we will meet again on the other side.

Harvey Drawdy and Kenneth Bryant.

Old #16

Kenneth and I mostly hunted squirrels and rabbits. Occasionally, we deer-hunted together. It pretty much depended on what kind of dogs we had that determined the type of hunting we would do. For years, I had a good squirrel dog, so we hunted squirrels. I always liked coon hunting, but Kenneth never would go coon hunting with me. Once he told me that as a youngster, his dad carried him coon hunting and kept him out all night. He said he got cold, wet, and sleepy, and that it was the most miserable night of his life. That one night broke him from ever wanting to coon hunt again. It didn't stop him from helping me skin out coons or helping me cook coons. He just wouldn't go hunting for coons at night. When we were neighbors and both raising a family, our hobbies always came second to our families, meaning we didn't have a lot of money to spend on our hobbies. So we made do with what we had, in terms of guns, dogs, and gear. That brings me to this story. Kenneth had an old sixteen-gauge shotgun. It was an old hand-me-down gun that one of his uncles gave him as a boy. That old gun killed a lot of squirrels and rabbits over the years, but it had started developing a mind of its own. Sometimes, it was hard to open, sometimes hard to close. Shells would get stuck in the barrel, and he would have to pry them out with a pocketknife. The gun was a double-barrel, and sometimes, it would shoot both barrels at the same time. Once we had gotten up very early and gone down to Edwards Swamp to hunt squirrels. We got there before daylight and turned the dog out. Kenneth loaded both barrels of Old #16 and snapped the gun barrels back in place, and the gun fired both barrels at the same time, barely missing my legs as I stood there beside him.

Potluck and Roadkill Café

One thing about Kenneth and me was that we didn't waste any of the game that we caught or killed. Most Saturdays, after our hunting or fishing trip, you could find us out in the shop cooking whatever game we had harvested that day. We both enjoyed cooking and eating, so cooking the game was natural to us. Here were some of the most common things cooked up in my café/shop…squirrels, rabbits, quail, doves, duck, deer, and fish of all types. Occasionally, we would offer a much more exotic menu, such as rattlesnake, alligator, possum, coon, carp, mudfish, and sheepshead that we caught in Georgetown at the Winyah Bay jetties. Other than one of these items considered the main entree, our menu would, more than likely, include some type of potato dish (usually panfried) and a slice of light bread, garnished with a few of Lottie's or Merle's homemade pickles. If a person happened to drop in on a Saturday afternoon, they were likely to be given a free dinner, whether they wanted it or not. It was difficult to get Merle and Lottie to join us. The kids usually dined with us, especially Patricia.

Old Cluck

One Easter, Merle let the boys get chickens for pets. Back then, baby chicks were dyed different colors and sold at Easter. I guess dying them different colors had something to do with dying eggs for Easter as well. The reality is that chickens and eggs have nothing to do with Easter Sunday; Easter is about the Risen Savior Jesus and how He died on the Cross for us all and then arose on the third day to defeat death. Regardless of the thought behind baby chicks, we had two of them to deal with. Over a short time, one of the chicks went on to chicken glory, but the other one survived and grew into a big full-grown rooster. His dyed color had faded, and now the rooster was completely white…and he thought he was a dog. He followed the boys around with the dog, and he ate from the dogs' bowl and drank from the dogs' water dish. I really think that he thought he was just like our other pets which were dogs. And he got along great with the dogs. The only things different about Ole Cluck and the dogs were that he clucked and crowed instead of barking, and he roosted instead of laying down in Merle's flower beds. And guess where he roosted…right on the trunk of Kenneth's blue Pontiac.

Now for one of the funniest stories I can tell about my best friend Kenneth. Most mornings when Kenneth came out and cranked his car, Cluck would jump off the back of the car and run back over to our house. Like the average family on Greenway Drive, the Bryant family only had one car. Lottie was a nurse, and she often worked second shift at the medical clinic. On the second shift, she got off just before midnight, and Kenneth would pick her up from work. This one particular night, things got slightly altered. Kenneth got into his car, cranked it, and took off. He never noticed ole Cluck standing on the back of his car flapping his wings and clucking as loudly as he could. As Kenneth got near the clinic, he slowed the car down and stopped, and that ole rooster jumped off the back of the car and began to run. The rooster ran up Pearl Street and darted into the police station and then onto the playground at the recreation center, and Kenneth was right behind him. Can you imagine Kenneth chasing that chicken…? He had to have looked a bit like Rocky Balboa trying to catch that chicken in the pen that Manager Mickey had set up to help Rocky gain speed before facing Apollo Creed in the ring. Somehow, Kenneth found his speed and was able to catch Cluck and bring him home. No one could tell that tale better than Kenneth. We had many laughs about the midnight ride of Ole Cluck.

The Price of Honey

After we moved away from Greenway Drive, Kenneth would come out to the house pretty regularly. That's where we did a lot of our huntin', fishin', cookin', gardenin', and tale tellin'. We also did a good bit of thinkin' back then, mostly about new adventures and new things to do. One day, we got to talking about the price of honey. Kenneth said that we could get all the honey we wanted for free because there were a couple of old beehives on his dad's farm down by the pond. So we jumped in the truck and rode over to see if they were active. We got there, and you could see bees swarming all around the two wooden hives. We decided there must be two or three gallons of honey in each hive, so back to my shop we went. Our minds were now fully engaged in beehive robbing. We needed a viable plan, a beekeeper's suit, and something to put the honey in. We decided the plan would be the easy part, so we focused on the honey reservoir and the beekeeper's suit.

I reached up on the wall of my shop and grabbed a galvanized foot tub that was hanging face down on the shop wall. First problem solved…the honey reservoir. Problem two…the suit! We pulled out an old thick canvas tarp and some netting from my Boy Scout supplies. I took a safari-type hat and draped it with the netting to make the head-and-face protective covering. Then we made a huge poncho-like covering by cutting a slit in the tarp and sticking my head up through the slit. I found a thick pair of work gloves. We were starting to see the possibilities of just how this could work. Problem two solved.

Now for the plan. Keep in mind that man can make all the plans he wants, but God determines the outcome of those plans. I was going to be the robber, and Kenneth was going to be the getaway driver. The plan was simple—we back up to the hives, and I will knock the top off hive number one and dump the honey, comb and all into the reservoir…aka foot tub. Then I will do the same thing with hive number two—jump on the back of the truck, and my driver will drive me down the road as fast as possible and blow the bees away. So I put on my poncho and then my headgear and gloves and got in the truck bed. Kenneth backed up to the hives, and we did a countdown…3…2…1.

I knocked the lid off the hive, and the bees swarmed on me. Kenneth jumped in the truck and rolled up the windows, and the bees continued to swarm. I grabbed the hive with a giant bear hug and dumped the contents in the tub and then dropped the hive and moved to hive number two and knocked the top off. By now, the bees were under my clothing and completely covered the netting so thickly I could hardly breathe. I dumped the honey in the tub. I swatted bees, got stung, tried to breathe, and yelled, "Go," as loud and as often as I could. Finally, after about a mile and a half down Rhodes Community Road, the bees were gone, and I could breathe. I tapped on the cab of the truck, and Kenneth slowed down and stopped. As I removed my NONPROTECTIVE clothing, I noticed that in the reservoir were hundreds of dead bees floating in a quart of loose amber-colored honey and some dark discolored honeycomb. We spent the next hour picking the bees out of the honey. We got maybe a quart of honey for our troubles and decided that the price of honey should be at least $100 per pint!

Fran Wall Weaver

Our Neighborhood Part 5

Mary Anne Sansbury and Clevie

M ary Anne was our very own Wonder Woman! Our Go-To Person! She was Awesome! She could tackle anything and succeed. She was our Hero! You see, she was a physical education major and had a body that depicted it. While visiting her a few years back (2016), I asked her, "How in this world did you manage to lift both Johnny Truluck and Jim Dewitt at the same time before their boat crashed into the Spring Street bridge that spanned Swift Creek?" She had run from her home to the site, assessed the upcoming danger, stepped up on the bridge concrete ledge, and leaned her well-developed thighs against the wooden beam guard rail. I can still see her well-sculpted calves as she leaned forward to lift each of the boys with one hand simultaneously to safety. She simply sat the young fellas down on the bridge. Those adventurous thirteen-year-olds had escaped what would have been a fateful event. It all happened so quickly, and we kids knew we had witnessed a miracle. Mary Anne's response to my question as to how she had performed that miracle was "by the Grace of God." We had been on Holy Ground that day.

Mary Anne graciously hosted the Wall family when we moved to Greenway Drive (1954). Clevie was my first little girlfriend in the neighborhood, and Mary Anne frequently set us up to play on her screened-in-porch. We gobbled up her fresh-made popcorn and her grape Kool-Aid. We also celebrated birthday parties on the porch. Clevie had beautiful olive skin and naturally curly dark hair. My hair was straight, and Mama tried hard, but when she curled it, it just frizzed. Andy is one year younger than Clevie and me. He was celebrating his second birthday and definitely into eating his Happy Birthday treats.

I am proud to declare that Clevie and I have remained friends for sixty-seven years. We shared many birthdays and scouting events, and we were in each other's weddings. I treasure our time spent together. Mary Anne loved nature—woods, water, creeks, plants, flowers, trees, etc. She collected rocks, seashells, cones, and petrified wood. Now I am an addicted nature lover due to her influence. Best of all, she taught us to identify poison oak, poison ivy, and poisonous snakes. She could snare one of those snakes with her homemade device in a heartbeat. YIKES! (One of her favorite expressions.) She intended for us to be in the yard, in shape, and having fun as the Sansburys' backyard was set up with every kind of playground equipment available. Mothers would sit and visit while children had the time of their lives. Mary Anne could give Hercules a run for the money. She was strong! She mixed and poured concrete, laid bricks to create a sandbox, poured concrete tables and stools, built concrete steps with rock inlays that gave us access to the creek, poured bases for our footprints with petrified wood columns, made stepping-stones, and poured peach basket steps to help us over her backyard fence. (Today, one of Mary Anne's sandbox concrete tables and a stool are enjoyed by children in my neighborhood where they adorn our wooded Fairy and Pirate Garden. Even a large piece of her petrified wood welcomes you into the gated area near our cottage.) When preparing to leave for school, she would announce for us to "Head 'em Up. Move 'em Out." You remember—*Rawhide!* She was funny by always reminding us to squeeze the glass soda bottle to get the last drop of our drink!

Mary Anne made wine from her grapevines, and we ate grape jelly. She let Clevie and me in her kitchen to cook. Clevie knew how to cook; I just assisted when she made her fruitcake each year, a month before the holidays. She'd pour sherry from their family decanter over the cake, wrap it up, and place it in a dark place to age. Paul usually assisted with giving the cake another splash about two weeks later! My mother loved making Clevie a fresh coconut cake, and Clevie would make it a point to visit Mama each time she returned to the neighborhood. Mary Anne and big Mincy Copeland (you will remember there was a little Mincy) were our Girl Scout leaders from second grade till finishing high school—Troop 220. From our neighborhood, Barbara Welch, Clevie, Cynthia Smyre, and I benefited from their devotion. "You could tell a girl from 220. You could tell her by her walk. You could tell a girl from 220. You could tell her by her talk. You could tell her by her manners, by her appetite, and such. You could tell a girl from 220, but you could not tell her much." (This is our theme song composed by Mary Anne and Big Mincy.) She taught us to camp out, build a fire, cook over the fire, make lanyards, and knit.

She was talented; in fact, she knitted gifts for us—sweaters, socks, slippers, hats, scarves, and Christmas stockings. She made mother a little stocking seven inches in height and two inches wide with a Santa on it and the word "MA" at the top. She could not fit the word "Mother" on it. When I put it out each Christmas, I still think that "MA" is also the initials for "Mary Anne." She was creative—designing and making beautiful lamps from neighborhood cypress knees, cross necklaces, and her own uplifting spiritual stationary. She also created needlepoint "Jesus" bookmarkers. She was a Witness. You know I can still hear that rock-polishing machine running full-time on her side porch. I treasure and often wear the rock necklace she made for me. She was generous.

SHE TAUGHT US TO SWIM. Of all of her attributes, she explained to me her most valued lesson shared with others was being a Red Cross swimming instructor. She was adamant we would know the rules concerning water safety. Cyndie and I treasure the friendship Mary Anne and our mother shared as neighbors for sixty-two years. They were loyal to one another. Looking back, I have to say Mary Anne saved darling Johnny Truluck and Jim Dewitt. Clevie saved me in the Copeland farm pond. Andy is a doctor, Danny has been a pastor for forty years, and Suzie is a missionary. The Sansburys were and are in the business of saving people!

Sunday Expectations

Our neighborhood was one of many faiths—Episcopalian, Methodist, Presbyterian, Baptist, etc. Religious influence caused us to hold our own little neighborhood church services where we passed a pretend collection plate and received a few coins as well as rocks, acorns, etc. This was also a time to baptize all of our baby dolls. In the Wall home, the Bible and Upper Room Devotional had a permanent place on the kitchen table. We were members of Trinity UMC. Mother did not believe in missing Sunday School or the Sunday worship service. And we even went back for MYF and Sunday evening services, as well as Wednesday nights. As my sister Cyndie says, "We were front row, center—piano side." If we misbehaved in church—a little giggle or whisper—it called for an afternoon of time-out on our twin beds. It is hard to walk around on a twin bed when you have a doll bed, high chair, baby dolls, etc. atop the mattress. During our punishment time, when gardenias were in bloom, Mother pretended not to notice when we raised our window, unlocked the screen, and picked gardenias to put on our pillows. (During blooming season, Mother always kept one of these flowers on the living room mantel.) Sometimes, she would get so exasperated with us on our beds we would receive a reduction in our sentencing and be sent to the yard to play. (Yeah, right where we longed to be!) You should also know, as young children, we were not allowed to play cards, roller-skate, or dance on the Sabbath. (By the way, as teens, when making new friends at the beach and being asked where we went to school, our response was St. John's High. Immediately, they assumed we were enrolled in a private Catholic school.)

Veterans

The stunning presence of a man in a military uniform could be seen almost daily in our neighborhood. James "Jabo" A. Powers could be observed arriving home to his pretty girls, dressed either in his green class A or class B Army apparel. The Greenway Drive area was "chock-full" of military veterans who wore the uniform of the various services at some time. Their commitment to God and country protected the everyday freedoms we young folks were able to enjoy. We were proud to learn patriotic songs when the different Armed Forces bands entertained us at St. John's High School auditorium. Paul Sansbury was a veteran and an American Legion member of Darlington Post 13. In 1946, he was one of four attendees who participated at the Arlington National Cemetery interment of the cremated remains of World War II Army Air Corps pilot and Darlington native Billy Farrow (one of Doolittle's Raiders).

Keith Carter

Mudslinging

O ne day, I was walking home from "Glory Hole," as my mother
called it. Glory Hole was the name for anywhere we wanted
to be that wasn't home. We lived near the Spring Street end of
Greenway, which wasn't very exciting, and I had been somewhere
playing toward the other end where all the fun was. When I got to
the Bonnoitts' house, Punk called to me from the front yard. "Hey,
come here!" Of course, I did—why not? It was when the Powers
were building their new house beside the Bonnoitts and across the
street from us, and there was an excellent muddy area beside the
Bonnoitts' house.

He said, "Let's throw mud on our house." Being a year older but
hardly any wiser, I told him I didn't think that was a very good idea.
It was the kind of thing parents usually didn't like. Punk said, "Oh,
my parents won't mind one bit. They don't care at all about stuff like
that." I was very skeptical, but, hey, it was his house and his parents
and him calling the shots, and it did sound like fun. Just to prove
his intentions, he picked up a hefty glob of mud and smacked it up
against the end of their white house. I watched as he flung another
glob; and I decided if he was going to do it, with or without me, I
would not be a bystander.

We got into it, and did we ever plaster that wall! We did avoid
the windows, but we didn't stop until the wall was totally covered in
mud, as far up as we could hit. It didn't take very long, and it was a
job well done. We rinsed our hands in a mudhole and bid each other
a fond farewell. What a friend!

As I walked into the house, Mother was on the phone in the kitchen, saying, "Okay, Nonie, I am terribly sorry. Yes, I most certainly will! Bye now." She hung up the phone and looked at me with her hands on her hips. "Did you and Punk just throw mud on the side of their house?" Uh oh, Punk was wrong when he said his parents wouldn't care about it one bit. "Yes, ma'am, but he said it was okay! He said his parents wouldn't care!" "Well, Nonie does care, and she said she's wearing Punk out and thinks I should wear you out too! You're older and should know better!" This was not going well at all.

My mother knew me pretty well. I was a fun-loving real boy, but I was also honest, and I was telling the truth. She asked me to tell her exactly what had happened, so I told her how Punk had beckoned me off the street to partake in the mudslinging. I told her I thought we shouldn't, but Punk said it wouldn't be a problem for his folks, and when he started doing it, I helped him.

She believed me, which I appreciate to this day. She had to follow up with spanking me since she had given her word to Nonie that she would, but it was a light one. Her heart wasn't in it. Years later, she told me she understood how much fun throwing mud like that would have been. But she said to follow my good sense and conscience, that if something seems wrong, don't do it, even if others are doing it. I was blessed in a lot of ways, and one was having a mother who put the right things into us, but she still remembered what it was like to be a child!

Stan Drawdy

Relics from the Past

O ne thing that you can say about Greenway Drive is that Scouting was alive and well in our neighborhood. Many of the boys and girls on our street were involved in a Scout troop. One of the Boy Scout troops actually met on Greenway Drive, every week at the Spooky Ole Barn; I believe Mr. Brunson was one of the leaders of that troop. My dad, Harvey, also had a troop that met at First Baptist Church once a week. Then there were at least two Cub Scout troops on our street. Mrs. Mary Anne Sansbury was the leader of one troop that met at her house, and Mrs. Jackie Sansbury (Pete and Jeff's mom) had a troop that met at her house. I know that there were several girls in the neighborhood involved in Girl Scouts of America, but I do not recall who their leaders were or where they met. I do know that the younger girls were called Brownie Scouts and the older group were Girl Scouts. There must have been lots of the girls involved, because I can remember Mom buying boxes and boxes of those delicious Girl Scout cookies every year. My favorite was the peanut butter ones. Once I asked Mom why she bought so many, and she said because she couldn't say no to any of the girls in the neighborhood because it might hurt their feelings. Well, she said no to me and Ricky all the time, whether it hurt our feelings or not. The point is, we had lots of cookies every year which must have translated into lots of Girl Scouts in the neighborhood selling them.

Almost all of the boys in our neighborhood were either Boy Scouts or Cub Scouts. One of my best playmates and friends was Jeff Sansbury, and I joined his mom's troop. We met at their house, and she always had

213

things planned for us to do. She would take us on trips. Once we toured a hospital. Once we combined with the other neighborhood troop and went to Lake Darpo where many of us earned a merit badge for the mile swim. Sometimes, we just stayed at her house and worked on our pledges and mottos, or did some arts-and-crafts-type stuff. I remember one time we made homemade taffy. One time, close to Christmas, we went into the woods and collected all-natural things from the woods to make Christmas decorations. I remember I used a piece of an old pine tree limb, drilled a hole in it, and stuck a candle in the drilled-out hole. Then I glued leaves on the small log and dripped colorful candle wax all over it. It was a perfect, all-natural (except for the candle) candleholder. Mrs. Jackie was a good Cub Scout leader.

These smiling Darlington Boy Scouts were not quite so dry when they returned (a few hours early) from a weekend camping trip to the Smoky Mountains.

Leaving Darlington at 2 p.m. Friday, the group camped Friday night in Pisgah National Forest, N. C., where they toured the fish hatchery. Then on Saturday they visited Ghost Town and Cherokee Indian Reservation and camped Saturday night at Round Bottom.

On the front row in this photograph taken just prior to their departure are, left to right, Stanley Drawdy, Mitchell Pottoff and Ricky Drawdy. Back row in the same order are Jimmy Shelley, Johnny Bonnoitt, Johnny Truluck, Jimmy Bonnoitt, Bill Hobbs, Ervin Law and Scoutmaster Harvey Drawdy. (Photo for The News and Press by Taft Michau).

Mr. Drawdy and Boy Scouts.

Girl and Boy Scout troops are not the only relics of the past. Many churches are closing their doors across this country. Whoever thought we would ever see "For Sale" signs in front of churches. Back then, we learned in school that this country was founded on the idea of freedom of religion. Schools taught us that we were lucky to be in this country and to be able to worship God without fear of being prosecuted. On Sunday mornings, church parking lots were full, and our neighborhood driveways were empty. Christianity and patriotism were our protected rights and our duty as Americans. Nowadays, these are both under attack by those who want to fundamentally change our country. On Greenway Drive, our parents and our friends' parents all worked together to teach us the values and norms that made this country great. Parents have "given back" by volunteering to be Scout leaders, Sunday school teachers, youth sports coaches, crossing guards, PTA members, and many other services, expecting nothing in return. Our Greenway Drive adults did their part in passing on the values of our nation. Sadly, my generation and those behind have fallen asleep at the wheel. Slowly but surely, the winds of change are turning the cornerstones of our culture into old relics of the past. Christianity, Patriotism, Giving Back, and Living the American Dream. The same ideals that made Greenway Drive the Greatest Place on Earth to Grow Up are what made America the Greatest Country in the World—Fearing God, Pride in our Country, loving others enough to Give Back without expectations, and Living the American Dream by Believing in Yourself enough to know you can be anything you want to be if you work hard enough for it.

One of my favorite TV shows is *American Pickers*. They go around the country looking for treasures in antique stores and junkyards. Their job is to find old relics from the past and restore them before they are lost forever. I think it's time we all stand up and become American Pickers and restore the relics of our past before they are lost forever.

That Guy

Greenway Drive was a great place to make friends. And the good thing about true friendship is…it lasts forever. I was fortunate that I developed many close friends in the ten years we lived on Greenway Drive. And to this day, they all remain good friends. Many I have not seen in years, but I know without a doubt that I could call on them if I needed help and they would be there for me, and I would be there for them too. One of my closest friends lived on Greenway Drive for only about a year. His family bought a lot over in the Country Club section of Darlington, and they were building a house there. They rented a small house on Greenway Drive for about a year, while they built the home on their lot. They lived in the house right in front of the "Spooky Barn."

I had known Mitch Mims prior to them moving to Greenway Drive. We had played recreation ball against each other for several years and had even been on the same all-star baseball team in Dixie Youth. Mitch was a year older than me and a full grade ahead of me in school. We both played second base, and we competed for the position on the all-star team. Mitch won the starting position (his dad was one of the coaches…Haha). Even through that, we became closer friends. Once he moved to my neighborhood, we became really close friends. You might even say he was the closest thing I ever had to a "big brother." That was a great year when he lived on Greenway Drive. Not long after Mitch's family moved away, my family moved also, out to Rhodes Community Road. Once we hit junior high, we stayed connected right on up through high school. We played ball together, had classes together, double-dated, and spent a lot of time together, just being teenagers. I think I was a better influence on Mitch than he was on me. I still give him credit for instigating most of the things that got me in trouble. Most of those things were fairly harmless, but I can think of a couple that will remain secrets between the two of us…and possibly one or two other friends.

Once a group of us decided to ride our Kawasaki 90s to the beach after prom. Mitch and I were the only ones who rode them home because everyone else blew their engines and had to catch rides home. On the way home, we stopped in Marion at some burger shack, and I couldn't get my bike cranked back up. Finally, after pushing and kick-starting, it fired up, and we took off. We made it to Darlington. Just as I pulled into my parents' driveway, my bike shut off. I had burned up the piston. Mitch's bike was the only one that didn't tear up. He was also the only one of us who only weighed eighty pounds, soaking wet.

After college, we sort of drifted apart, but we would occasionally contact each other to catch up. Mitch became a businessman and then a realtor. I went into coaching and later into real estate investing. We went many years without much contact, except on my birthday. Every year on my birthday, Mitch would call me. He has done that for as long as I can remember. I called him a time or two on his birthday, but apparently, I'm not as good at remembering dates as Mitch.

Not too long ago, I heard that Mitch's daughter, Heather, was going through treatments for cancer. I reached out to Mitch about her, and he told me that she was actually doing pretty well. Not long after that, I heard that Mitch was in the same battle that his daughter had been through. He told me that he had completed his first round of chemo and that the results showed that he wasn't better, but he wasn't worse either. The cancer was still there, and they would try plan B. He also said that he and both his kids were taking a trip to the Keys and to Key Largo for a getaway. I told him to check out Isle of Marada while in the Keys and to send me some photos from the trip. About a week later, Heather sent me a string of photos from the trip. A couple of days after that, Mitch contacted me and said, "I'm coming to get you. We are going to Darlington." The next Monday morning, Mitch met me at Pamplico Motors; and I gave him a tour of my sanctuaries…the football stadium, the farm, the lake, and my cabin. Then we headed to Darlington. As we rode, we talked and caught up on everything from bootleggers to kicking out nightlights, and in no time, we were mentally back on Greenway Drive…two old men reliving our youth. We talked about the people, places, and events that had been buried in our subconscious for all those years.

Where had the time gone? When we got to Darlington, we stopped at Taki's for lunch, hoping to run into some old friends; and we did. We prayed together before lunch, asking God to be with Mitch and to see him and his family through this hard, stressful time and terrible illness. We thanked God for all our blessings, blessings that we probably didn't deserve, and asked forgiveness from our sins. At that moment, I knew that we were not just great friends but brothers in Christ. Even with all our mistakes and shortcomings in life, God was there with us. After lunch, we hit the reminiscence trail… the old St. John's High School, Dixie Youth field at Brunson-Dargan (which is no longer there. Only the backstop remains), the football stadium (bleachers are gone), baseball stadium, Spring Street, and Greenway Drive. Then we drove over to Bryan and Patricia Hobbs' house and spent a couple of hours with Bryan. We toured their newly renovated home. How awesome it is.

On the way back to Pamplico, Mitch asked me if we ever got any Fiats on our car lot. I said, "Nope, we ain't that kind of car lot. Think cheaper!" Then he said, "Well, I am in the market for one. I am going to be 'that guy.'" I laughed. The next day, he sent me a photo of him sitting in a white 2018 Fiat convertible. I thought, *You go, boy!* One might think that Mitch has made out his bucket list and he has certain things he wants to accomplish before his time runs out…and maybe there is some truth to that, but I do not think so. What I see is that Mitch has realized that he is going to spend the rest of his days living his life to the fullest. None of us know how many days we have left. You don't have to have a disease to let you know how fragile life on earth is. Mitch has figured out the secret to life—you live it and live it large. We all need to do as Tim McGraw says in his song—"Live each day like you are dying."

"That Guy," Mitch Mims.

And that takes me back to Greenway Drive. A time when every day was a blessing, a gift from God. A time where God, family, and friends were the most important things in life. A time when we lived every day as if it were our last, trying to fit in as much fun in a day as possible. A time where we believed we could do anything and that we were invincible. Catching live snakes, cruising down and around suicide hill on a homemade skateboard, climbing the Naked Tree, conquering the Spooky Old Barn, smoking rabbit tobacco, ice-skating on Kilgos' Pond, racing bicycles, riding no-hands down Spring Street hill, playing full-tackle football with no pads and no helmets, and running behind the mosquito truck breathing in all the smoke.

Life can be hard. There is a lot of negativity going on in our world today, and it is easy to become stagnant and cynical. It is easy to wish your life away, waiting for something good to happen or waiting on some sort of changes to occur. Thanks to my buddy Mitch Mims, I can see that we should live like each day will be the last. Love the Lord with all our heart, soul, and mind; and love our neighbors as we love ourselves. And as John Wooden said, "Make each day a masterpiece." Then approach life with the attitude of a kid from Greenway

Drive! And maybe, just maybe in doing these things, you might just find out that you can be "that guy" too.

Postscript

On February 23, 2022, my very good friend Mitch Mims went home to be with our Lord. I will always remember Mitch as one of my lifelong friends. He and his family lived on Greenway Drive for a short time when he was a kid, which was when Mitch and I became close friends. We played and learned together during that year. As teens, we grew up together; as adults, we matured together; and as senior citizens, we became old men who reminisced and prayed together. In one of our last conversations, Mitch told me that his battle with cancer took its toll on him mentally and physically. He told me how much he loved his family, and he hated the thought of leaving them behind. But he looked forward to seeing his mom and dad again.

For those of us who, like Mitch, put our faith and hope in Jesus Christ, there is no death—only the transition from this life into eternal life. Mitch will be missed by those of us who knew and loved him, but he will never be forgotten. And we will see him again when our Lord and Savior calls us home to be with Him.

Fran Wall Weaver

Blessed

S ometimes, we are given unexpected but timely, precious, divine, life-changing gifts—ones which create a safe passage forward and shape and mold our lives. That is exactly what our neighborhood provided the Wall family while living both on Greenway Drive in 1954–1955 and returning to live on Evans Circle in 1957. Tell me, where else could two children live and have neighbors put their Christmas gifts together at the midnight hour while their dad was serving overseas? Then, after their father has passed away and they have moved back into the neighborhood, have those two neighbors, Johnny Bonnoitt and Jimmy Brown, come again every Christmas morning for years to see what Santa has delivered? And take time to have coffee, with a piece of our mother's delicious fresh-made coconut cake or a homemade fried apple pie? How very dear their precious wives and children were to share them with us. I must tell you, I treasure my childhood days and memories where happiness stays close to me no matter where I am. All of my life, my precious mother said to Cyndie and me, "I am so BLESSED." Our entire family was abundantly blessed as we experienced a bit of Heaven on Earth living in the Greenway Drive area.

Virginia S. Howell

A Wonderful Neighborhood

My husband, Brastice, and I were married in 1948 and lived in several apartments around Darlington before moving to our new house on Spring Street Extension around 1950. This was an exciting step in our lives, and this was the only house we would ever own. I was raised in a loving home in Darlington Mill Village while my husband was raised in a loving farmer's home in several houses around Darlington County. Our home was built in a new housing project that was established right next to the beautiful Williamson Park. Our neighborhood grew very quickly, with many new houses and families making their homes on Greenway Drive, Spring Street Extension, Pinehaven Avenue, and Evans Street. This was a perfect place to live and raise a family in the '50s and '60s. These were homes well-suited for young couples starting their lives together and raising their children. The houses filled up quickly, children soon appeared, friendships were established, and life was good. It was a safe place where children played and roamed without fear unless they were caught misbehaving. It was generally understood a parent of one was a parent of all if any necessary, but loving disciplinary measures were required. The children got along very well. They shared their school years and summers and made many lasting friendships.

I will soon turn ninety-four and still live in the same little house on Spring Street that Sammy and Keith grew up in. They had a wonderful neighborhood in which to experience their childhood. They grew up under the watchful eyes of so many good and caring adults and with so many good friends their age. Of course, the neighborhood children eventually grew up, and many left to go their separate ways. Still, it always warms my heart each time I see or hear from those who stayed, those who return to stay, and those who visit if only for a short time. They return to renew friendships, comfort and help friends, remember a friend, remind themselves of their roots, or make Darlington their home again. I can look back with fond memories of our times together when traffic was never a problem and neighbors knew and took care of each other and lived life at what appears now to have been a much simpler, kinder, and slower pace. At the same time, I am blessed and grateful to still be here in the neighborhood with good and caring friends and neighbors where it all started many years ago. I treasure my time in the little red house on Spring Street and each and every one of you who have impacted my life in such a fulfilling way.

*****

Authors' Note: Mrs. Howell passed away on January 17, 2022, before this book went to press. Thanks to Fran Wall Weaver and Barbara Truluck Benjamin, we have the handwritten note that Mrs. Howell wrote for the Greenway Drive Reunion that was held October 2017 and was read at the reunion.

I, Jenny Howell, send best wishes to the children of this neighborhood. All took different paths but always made it back to support one another at reunions, weddings, funerals, or just to comfort. I think the parents sent you all out to make the world a better place. Thanks for the memories of you.

Trust the Lord with all thine heart; and lean not unto thine own understanding. In all thy ways acknowledge Him, and He shall direct thy paths. Proverbs 3:5–6 (KJV)

This passage of scripture was mentioned and quoted at Mrs. Howell's funeral.

The End

About the Contributors

Barbara Truluck Benjamin
Barbara still lives on Greenway Drive in Darlington and is married to Chesley. They have two children and six grandchildren. She is a lifelong member of the First Baptist Church of Darlington. Barbara thanks God for all the families and lasting friendships in this neighborhood.

Jim Brown
Jim(bo) and his wife, Michal "Sis" Baird from Darlington, live on Sullivan's Island, South Carolina. They have one son, Baker. Jim paints under the name Jim Darlington, and his landscapes and portraits can be seen in galleries in Charleston.

Keith Carter
Keith lives in Greenville, South Carolina, and has been married for fifty years to Tonda, a retired educator. His first career was mortgage lending, and his second career (since 1996) is remodeling contractor. He has two daughters and three grandchildren. (Email: ktcarter116@hotmail.com)

Clevie Sansbury Daniels
Clevie lives in Michigan and has been married for forty-eight years to Tony (retired USAF colonel and UPS pilot). They have three (married and employed) children and seven grandchildren. (Email: clevie@sbcglobal.net)

Harvey and Merle Drawdy
Harvey and Merle live in Darlington, South Carolina, and both retired from Darlington County Schools—him as an elementary principal, and her as a school secretary.

Stan Drawdy
Stan, DEd, is a retired high school football coach and athletic administrator, also a national faculty member of US Sports Academy, and lives in Pamplico, South Carolina. (Email: raidercoach99@ yahoo.com)

Cynthia Wall Geries
Cyndie lives in Hartsville, South Carolina. She's a retired educator and School District Attendance Supervisor. (Email: cgeries@ gmail.com)

Peggy Melton Greene
Peggy is retired and lives in Florence, South Carolina, but she has always stayed close to her hometown, Darlington.

Barbara Welch Haynes
Barbara, a happily retired educator, lives in Darlington, South Carolina, and is married to her high school sweetheart, Randy Haynes. She has two sons, three grandchildren, and four bonus children (one is deceased). (Email: blwh52@gmail.com)

Sammy L. Howell
Sammy resides in Cross Hill, South Carolina, with his wife, Ann Pridgen Howell, who is also from Darlington. He retired as a professor of Economics and Business Administration at Presbyterian College. Ann is a retired guidance counselor and teacher. (Email: slhowell52@gmail.com)

Virginia Howell
Virginia "Jenny" Shepard Howell was married to her husband, Brastice (1925–2012). She purchased a new Spring Street house

around 1950 and never left. She had two sons, Sammy and Keith. She worked ten years at Rose's Dime Store and retired from Nytronics.

Bobby Kilgo
Bobby lives in Darlington, South Carolina, and is married to Sue. His first career was as an attorney, also taught at Florence-Darlington Technical College. He's currently an economic development director for Darlington County. (Email: robertkilgo@att.net)

Robin Mills
Robin lives in Irmo, South Carolina, and is married to Mike Sterling. She is retired from working with the United States Department of Justice. (Email: Rmx01@aol.com)

Mitchell Mims
Mitch lived in Murrells Inlet, South Carolina, married to Donna, and was a Realtor for The Litchfield Company.

Danny Sansbury
Danny is the third child of Paul and Mary Anne Sansbury, is married to Joye, and lives in Hartsville, South Carolina. He graduated from St. John's High, USC, and Columbia Seminary. He pastored churches in North Carolina, Tennessee, and South Carolina before retiring.

Dane Smyre Jr.
Dane is a retired social worker living and playing golf in Tucson, Arizona, and is married to Kim Murphy of Butte, Montana, for forty-five years. (Email: desmyre@q.com)

Sarah Cain Spruill
Sarah lives in Cheraw, South Carolina—the hometown of her husband, James A. Spruill. She has been active in preservation and heritage tourism. They have two daughters: Sarah, an attorney in Greenville, and Calder, an architect in Asheville, North Carolina.

Gregg Suggs

Gregg lives in Darlington, South Carolina, is married to Lisa, and owns Suggs Insurance Agency. (Email: suggsinsurance@aol.com)

Ingram Truluck

Ingram lives in Florence, South Carolina, and is married to Cheri with three children and two grandchildren. His first career was in radio broadcasting, and second was as a registered nurse. He's a member of Florence Baptist Temple, Marine Corps League, and Marine Corps Heritage Foundation.

Fran Wall Weaver

Fran lives in Hartsville, South Carolina; is married to Grady, a Sonoco retiree; utilized her interior design degree over the years while living in four different states; and has one daughter and one grandson.

CPSIA information can be obtained
at www.ICGtesting.com
Printed in the USA
BVHW010236060123
655681BV00005B/149